The Ultimate Prepper Collection
Survival Guides For Every Situation

By Robert Paine

© 2014

All rights reserved. No part of this publication may be reproduced, distributed, or transmitted in any form or by any means, including photocopying, recording, or other electronic or mechanical methods, without the prior written permission of the publisher, except in the case of brief quotations embodied in critical reviews and certain other noncommercial uses permitted by copyright law.

And above all – Enjoy!

Table of Contents

Prepping 101: A Beginner's Survival Guide

Prepper's Pantry: A Food Survival Guide

The Nomad Prepper: A Guide to Mobile Survival

Prepping with Children: A Family Survival Guide

Prepping 101: A Beginner's Survival Guide

Introduction

Have you watched the news lately? Most people would agree that the world has become a pretty scary place. There are natural disasters on an almost daily basis, we are running out of natural resources, our food is full of chemicals, and the ozone looks like Swiss cheese. There are threats of wars, terrorist attacks and jokes about zombie's taking over. The world economy is crumbling and we certainly can't depend on the government to help us out. They've "shut down" until they come to some sort of agreement over a hundred different issues on their plates, and, (let's be real here) the government hasn't agreed on much of anything since the Declaration of Independence was first signed. It's enough to send a person into a panic, isn't it?

If you are reading this, then you are among one of the many who are interested in learning how to protect yourself and your family from any and all of the inevitable disasters that could potentially happen. Welcome to the Survivor Family. We are a unique group of people. Some people call us Survivalists, Paranoid Crackpots, Doomsday Preppers, or Patriots. Whatever you may want to call yourself, if you're reading this, you are on the first step to becoming an Emergency Prepared Survivor (EPS).

If this is the first time you are reading anything about Emergency Preparation, **the first thing you need to know is: Don't Panic.** Being calm and using your training is one of the best weapons you have, but common sense is often the first thing people lose in an emergency situation.

Being prepared is really not as complicated as a lot of people make it out to be. This beginner's guide will take you step-by-step through the process of preparing for anything from a simple power outage to what you need to do to be prepared to evacuate your home and live outdoors indefinitely. At the end of this book, you will find a list of supplementary books I highly recommend to purchase. No one book will ever cover the dozens of things you'd hope to know in a survival situation, and anyone that tells you otherwise simply wants you to buy *something*. Take a look at the recommend books, if you wish, and *I suggest you read them before you need them.* For now, all you need to know is the most basic of survival skills: Thinking like a survivor, and learning how to obtain water, shelter, fire and food – the four basics survival needs. You'll learn what tools you need and what to do in case of a basic medical emergency, as well as two of the most common forms of communication in survival situations.

Needing to know what to do in an emergency situation is a lot easier if you've studied the basics before the actual emergency occurs. In the next chapters, you will find the fundamental rules of basic survival, put in simple terms that even the most novice of beginners can understand and implement. For the more experienced EPS, this book may seem extraordinarily simple; however, you may find a few nuggets of wisdom, or a new method you've never thought about in quite the same way and, remember, we all had to start somewhere! As the saying goes, knowledge is power, and the more knowledge you accumulate, the more powerful your arsenal of survival techniques will be.

Some of you may be wondering what qualifies me, of all people, to be teaching you about survival. I grew up in a Survivor Family. My father taught me and my brothers, since the time we were born, how to survive in a vast majority of situations. He wanted to make sure that, if anything were to ever happen to him, that we could all take care of ourselves. With over twenty years of camping trips, Scouts, and Search and Rescue training, I've learned a thing or two about how to live and survive with minimal modern conveniences and supplies. As an avid reader, I've gained even more knowledge of various aspects of survival over the years, and I learn more every day from other EPS's.

That being said, I'm not the most prepared person on the planet. I don't live up in the mountains in a remote cabin a thousand miles from my nearest neighbor. I'm not writing to you from an underground bunker somewhere, waiting for the world to explode.

I imagine I am just like most of my readers. I live in a simple home, doing the best I can to protect my family "just in case" the worst-case scenario actually happens. Because it has happened to other people and it could happen to you to.

Chapter 1: The Psychology of Survival
A New Way of Thinking

The best EPS is someone who can analyze a situation, adapt to a situation and act accordingly. For some people, these skills come naturally, but for most of us, it requires a new way of thinking. Human beings are creatures of habit and this is especially true of our methods of mental processing and behavior. In an emergency situation, you need to learn how to think like a survivor. It's best to begin thinking in terms of survival before you actually need to, so that you have the time you need to adjust to a new way of living.

You may be asking yourself, what it is you are supposed to be adjusting to? The answer is simple. *Learning to survive is about learning to live without everything you have grown to depend on to always be there.* Being forced to live without the everyday comforts we are used to can create a lot of stress on a person, physically, emotionally and mentally. Before you will understand psychological reactions in a survival setting, it is important to know how stress affects people.

Stress is not a disease that you cure, but is something that needs to be eliminated from your everyday life. It's not something you can avoid completely in life, but there are certainly ways you can most effectively deal with it. It is a condition we all experience on some level or another. Stress is simply a reaction to pressure around us. Stress is just a word we use to describe the experiences we have in response to life's many tensions.

A Need for Stress

We need stress because it helps us to respond appropriately to certain situations. Stress provides us with challenges. It lets us know that something important is happening that we need to deal with. It gives us chances to learn about our values and strengths. How we handle stress shows us how we handle pressure and how we can succeed. Stress tests our adaptability. Contrary to popular belief, it is *not* always a negative thing. Stress can be a motivating force in your life, if you allow it to be. We need to have some stress in our lives, to keep us on our toes. The goal is to have stress, but not an excess of it. Too much stress can take its toll on people mentally and physiologically. Too much stress leads to distress. Distress causes an uncomfortable tension that we try to escape and avoid. Listed below are a few of the common signs of distress you may find in yourself or others.

- Angry outbursts.
- Low energy level.
- Constant worrying.
- Trouble getting along with others.
- Hiding from responsibilities.
- Carelessness.

- Forgetfulness.
- Depression and Withdrawal
- Making too many mistakes
- Difficulty making decisions.

Stress can be destructive if you let it. Or it can motivate you. It can encourage or discourage, and make life meaningful or meaningless. In a survival situation, you choose whether you will live or die. It is your ability to manage the stresses you will encounter that determines how successful you will be. A survivor is a person who works with the stress they encounter and who lets it build them up instead of break them down.

Survival Stressors
Any event can lead to stress and, as we've all experienced, stressful events don't always come one at a time in a nice, orderly fashion. Often, stressful events occur simultaneously. 'When it rains, it pours'. These events that produce stress are called "stressors." Stressors are the cause, and stress is the response. In response to a stressor, the body prepares either to "fight or flee." This preparation involves a cascade of chemical and physical triggers throughout the body. The body releases stored fuels (sugar and fats) to provide quick energy. Breathing increases to supply more oxygen to the blood while muscle tense to prepare for action. Blood clotting agents are activated to reduce bleeding while senses become heightened, so that you are more aware of your

surrounding. This protective posture lets a person cope with potential dangers that many people call an adrenaline rush. However, the body cannot maintain this level of alertness indefinitely. Prolonged stress reactions will cause health issues. The cumulative effect of minor stressors causes major distress if they all happen at the same time of if they are not dealt with properly. As the body's ability to handle stress wears down and the sources of stress increase, exhaustion occurs. When that happens, the ability to use stress positively goes away and distress starts to take a toll. The ability to anticipate key stressors and learning coping mechanisms for stress will allow a survivor to effectively manage the stress they are facing. It is essential for a survivor to be aware of the types of stressors they will encounter. The following are the most common:

Fatigue, Injury, Illness, or Death

Injury, illness, and death are real possibilities a survivor is forced to face. Nothing is more stressful than being in an unfamiliar, life-threatening environment. Illness and injury can limit your ability to maneuver, obtain enough food or water, build a proper shelter, and defend yourself, if you have to. Being sick or injured makes us feel vulnerable, and in a survivor situation, that feeling can increase under pressure. Forcing yourself to continue surviving is not easy as you grow more and more tired. It is possible to become so fatigued that the act of just staying awake becomes stressful. It is important for the survivor to have courage and persevere despite the possible risks.

Uncertainly and Lack of Control

Some people have trouble reacting in settings where everything is in chaos. Some people feel the need to be in constant control of the environment around them and, often in a survival situation, this is exactly the first thing people lose. Nothing is guaranteed in a survival situation, and that means a person is automatically uncertain and not in control. It can be extremely stressful operating on limited resources in unfamiliar settings. The stress of uncertainty takes a toll emotionally and psychologically.

Environment

Even under the most ideal circumstances, nature is your most formidable enemy. A survivor will have to contend with the stressors of the elements, their surrounding and the wildlife. Survivors' surroundings can be a source of food, shelter and protection from predatory animals, or it can be a source of stress, causing anything from mild discomfort to death. It all depends on your ability to stay calm and adapt to what is around you.

Hunger and Thirst

Without food and water, a person will eventually die. Obtaining and preserving food and water is one of the most important factors for a survivor to contend with. The longer you are out of your comfort zone (your home where food and water are readily available), the more important thirst and hunger become. For a person used to having his basic needs easily met from grocery stores or by popping open the fridge, foraging for food and water can be incredibly stressful.

Isolation

There are some advantages to facing adversity with others. As people, we have become used to the community, socialization and communication friends and family provide, especially during times of confusion. Being in contact with others also provides a greater sense of security. Help is available if problems happen. A significant stressor in survival situations is that a person has to rely on his or her own resources.

*****

The survival stressors mentioned in this section are by no means the only ones you may face. Remember, what is stressful to one person may not be stressful to another. Your experiences, training, personal outlook on life, physical and mental conditioning, and level of self-confidence contribute to what you will find stressful. The object is not to avoid stress, but rather to manage the stressors of survival and make them work for you.

Man has been able to survive many shifts in his environment throughout the centuries. His ability to adapt to a changing world kept him alive while other species died off. The same survival mechanisms can help keep us alive in our day and age as well. It is not surprising that the average person will have some psychological reactions in a survival situation. The important thing is how we choose to deal with them.

Are You Prepared to Live?
Your mission in a survival situation is simple: to stay alive. Fear, anxiety, anger, frustration, guilt, depression, and loneliness are all possible reactions to the many stresses common to survival. These reactions, when controlled in a healthy way, help to increase a person's likelihood of surviving. They prompt the person to pay more attention to their surroundings, to fight back when scared, to take actions that ensure sustenance and security, to keep faith and work with others in your family or group to make it through.

When the survivor cannot control their emotional reactions in a constructive way, these same emotions can easily bring him to a standstill. Instead of rallying his internal resources, the person listens to his internal fears and becomes paralyzed by them, unable to do what is necessary to survive. This creates psychological defeat long before he physically succumbs. Remember, survival is natural to everyone; however, being unexpectedly thrust into the life and death struggle is not. Prepare yourself to rule over these reactions so they serve your ultimate interest--staying alive.

This involves preparation to ensure that your reactions in a survival setting are productive, not destructive. The challenge of survival has produced countless examples of heroism, courage, and self-sacrifice. These are the qualities it can bring out in you if you have prepared yourself. Below are a few tips to help prepare yourself psychologically for survival. Once you learn them you can guide your family in adapting a survival attitude as well.

Know Yourself and Anticipate Your Fears
Through training, family and friends take the time to discover who you are on the inside. Strengthen your stronger qualities and develop the areas that you know are necessary to survive. Don't pretend that you will have no fears. Begin thinking about what would frighten you the most if forced to survive alone. Train in those areas of concern to you. Become comfortable dealing with areas where you recognize you have the biggest need. The goal is not to eliminate the fear, but to build confidence in your ability to function despite your fears.

Be Realistic
Don't be afraid to make an honest appraisal of situations. Survival is not a time to sugarcoat or gloss over anything. See your circumstances for what they are, not as you want them to be. Keep your hopes and expectations within the estimate of the situation. When you go into a survival setting with unrealistic expectations, you may be laying the groundwork for bitter disappointment.

Follow the adage, "Hope for the best, prepare for the worst." It is much easier to adjust to pleasant surprises about one's unexpected good fortunes than to be upset by one's unexpected harsh circumstances.

Train

Through military training and life experiences, using whatever means and methods are around you, begin today to prepare yourself to cope with the rigors of survival. Demonstrating your skills in training will give you the confidence to call upon them should the need arise. Remember, the more realistic the training, the less overwhelming an actual survival setting will be.

Learn Stress Management Techniques

People under stress have a potential to panic if they are not well-trained or if they are not prepared psychologically to face whatever the circumstances may be. While we often cannot control the survival circumstances in which we find ourselves, it *is* within our ability to control our response to those circumstances. Learning stress management techniques can significantly enhance your capability to remain calm and focused as you work to keep yourself and others alive. A few good techniques to develop include relaxation skills, time management skills, assertiveness skills, and cognitive restructuring skills (the ability to control how you view a situation).

Remember, "the will to survive" can also be considered to be "the refusal to give up."

Short Term Survival Mentality

What is short-term survival mentality? *Short term is anything from three days to three months.* Do you recall the disaster and chaos of Hurricane Katrina? A majority of those people were not prepared, and were forced to wait on FEMA and other organizations to supply them what they needed to survive. It was utterly horrible, and we learned something as a nation: sometimes in disaster scenarios, it's best to rely on yourself. *You need to be prepared to survive without any outside help for at least three months.* That means having enough water, food, and hygiene products, sources of heat and shelter for you and your family. Hint - Don't forget to plan ahead for your family pets. Even the most lovable dog or cat *will* become vicious if they are starving. Another thing to think about - Do you need medications? Make sure you have extras from your doctor. If you explain you are looking forward and preparing for a worst-case scenario situation, they may be willing to help you stock up on your basic medications. This is especially important for anyone with a chronic illness, like asthma, diabetes, epilepsy or someone with a heart condition. If you have allergies, you need to be sure you have enough medication on hand. Ideally, you should have a three-month supply.

The best way to discover how prepared you are, is to practice surviving without these items before you are actually forced to go without them. **Try this for a week: Turn off your electricity. Turn off your water. Can you and your family survive just seven days? Three days? Can you even make it through 24 hours?**

Do you have enough bottled water, nonperishable food, blankets, warm clothes, flashlights, candles, pet food, medications, toilet paper and diapers for the baby? Are you physically fit enough to walk to the store and carry fifty pounds of what you need all the way home? Are you prepared to live outdoors? How would your children react? How would *you* react? These are things an EPS learns to think about and prepare for. For now, just try to go one week without electricity. After a few days you'll learn really quickly what you really *need* and *what you can learn to live without*.

Most of us have become spoiled and lazy with all of our modern conveniences. From the moment we start our day we "need" electricity. The human race has survived throughout most of history without electricity, and you can do it too. You know - if you have to. At the bare minimum, a survivor should be prepared to live without the modern convenience of electricity. Whether it is a simple windstorm that kicks out a transformer, or a flood, earthquake or other natural disaster, electric power is usually one of the first things to go, and there is no telling when it might come back on. Is your family ready to survive without this one basic convenience? Better start preparing now.

In an effort to be prepared, figure out how much of everything essential you need for your family for one month, and multiply that by five. It's always good to have an extra months worth of supplies, in case things take longer to get back to normal, and another months worth of supplies if you need to barter for something you don't have. For example, if someone needs food, and you ran out of bandages or cough medicine, you can trade some of your extra food without worrying about your own family. Having more than you need is better than not having enough of what you need.

Be Prepared to Deal with Anything!
One of the biggest shocks for people forced to live in a survival situation is that they quickly realize they were ill prepared for the experience. They don't realize how much work it takes to do even the simplest things without modern conveniences and appliances. They don't realize how mentally and emotionally exhausting survival can be. That is why it is important to practice survivor skills ahead of time and to become comfortable working in those types of environments. Then, when needed, you'll have practical knowledge of survival skills at your disposal. How you think will

determine your success or failure, not only in life, but also in survival situations.

So, what *is* the first thing you should think about?

Stay calm. First and foremost, do not panic. People who panic do stupid things. Doing stupid things can get yourself or other people hurt. The calmer you are, the easier it will be to keep others calm. How do you be calm? Take a deep breath. Speak in a normal, relaxed tone, and stay positive. If you have young children, be sure that they do not see you freak out. It will only scare them and create more panic. No matter how scared you may be, it's your job to keep a cool head.

In a group, the calmest, most prepared, knowledgeable and rationally thinking person should be the leader that others are willing to follow. People in groups have a pack mentality, just like wolves in the wild. Someone has to be the alpha dog, and if you are the head of your family, that person should be you. If you want to make sure you are the leader in a crisis, then your family has to be clear on that role you play, every day, not just when bad things happen. In a chaotic survival situation, it is NOT a time for your spouse to demand their way or your kids to pitch a fit. Make sure they understand that such behavior won't be tolerated, and that everyone's survival depends on it. Your responsibility is to make sure everyone is taken care of. Above all, it's your job to make sure you follow the 3 S's:

1. Are my decisions ensuring the group's **safety**?
2. Is my home/shelter/camp **secure**?
3. Is my family prepared to **survive** and thrive?

Assess the situation. Figure out what the most pressing need is, and handle it. A lot of the time, survival is about living in the moment and doing what needs to be done before or as things come up. If the power goes out, for example, the most pressing need is obtaining a light source. To prepare for this eventuality, you need to have candles, lamps, or flashlights readily available. Know where they are and make sure you have what you need, whether it is extra wicks or extra batteries. Whatever the need is, it's up to you to deal with it as quickly and efficiently as possible.

Be a leader others look up to. A great leader can handle people diplomatically and learn to assess the group they are leading. If someone knows more about farming or emergency medicine than you do, delegate those responsibilities to the people who can best help the entire group. If you have children, make sure they feel included in the decision-making process whenever possible. Ask them about their ideas on how to do things. Even if you think you already know, making them feel important will help them to stay calm.

Children's brains solve problems differently than adults, and often their problem solving method is a common sense, simple solution. This creative attribute in children is what allows them to adapt and be resilient. Adults tend to over complicate things, while children see the problem and come up with the simplest solution possible. A great leader listens to all the people they lead. You never know where the best answer will come from.

Be smarter than the average monkey. When people panic, they don't think clearly. A lot of survival is about common sense. You need water, shelter, heat and food (in that order) to maintain life. Survival isn't about comfort. If it comes right down to it, everything else is not important. So, be smart about what you choose to add to your survival pack. If something doesn't fall into one of those four categories, leave it behind. Not many people know how to think like a survivor. They will take the things they *think* they can't live without; meanwhile, they won't have the things they actually need. Many comfort items are useless. The only exceptions are in children's Bug Out Bags (BOB's). If you have room for things like: a deck of cards, coloring books, crayons, or mini games, bring them, especially if you have children. Non-electronic forms of entertainment go a long way to combat utter boredom. When people get bored, they get crabby. You don't want cranky children when you are trying to survive a chaotic situation.

Have a Plan (and Plan Ahead)

Your plan for survival will change depending on the circumstances surrounding it. *Be Flexible!* The more prepared you are to deal with anything that comes up, the easier it will be for everyone to stay calm and rational. You don't want to add to the panic by being part of the masses that are unprepared and frantically ransacking stores for supplies. Have your supplies ready and plan ahead. If you live in the city, be ready to get out as fast as you can before looting and traffic jams make it impossible. Have a secondary location you are headed to out of the danger zone. If necessary, be prepared to leave the state. How do you know when it's time to get out?

I'm calling this the Survival Condition (SUVCON) Scale:

5. **Normal Conditions**: Regular day-to-day schedules followed. Preparations are made at leisure. There is nothing pressing to worry about at the moment, but the more prepared you are, the better off your family will be. Things you can do to be ready for anything:

- Continue stocking for food, medicine, and other supplies. Add items to your long-term shelter and your Bug Out Bag (BOB).
- Can and dehydrate as much food as you can. Store dry goods in freezer bags and put in waterproof Rubbermaid bins.

- Add money to your SHTF fund. Swap some of it out for gold. Watch the prices of gold. The higher the value per ounce, the more the economy is struggling.
- Invest in 5-gallon cans of gas. Fill them as often as you can afford.
- Consider swapping your electric stove for a propane gas stove, so that you have the ability to cook for your family when the power goes out.
- Make sure your home has properly insulated windows and doors. Have a supply of sandbags ready to go to block floodwaters.
- Replace batteries in fire alarms and other smoke alarms every six months.
- Have an emergency evacuation plan in case of fire.
- Make sure children know where they should meet you if they get split up, their parents' phone number, address, and emergency contact information.
- Invest in a set of cast iron cookware that can be used over an open flame, if necessary.
- Buy a pistol and learn to shoot. Have your kids learn too. It's not dangerous if you know the proper safety protocol. It doesn't matter what political views you have. You are in a life or death situation and no one else will care if you like guns or not. If you want to live, you will need to be able to defend your family.
- Take a self-defense course and an emergency first aid course.

- Make sure your kids learn to swim. Get them involved in Scouts or some equivalent to teach them basic outdoor survival skills and so they will learn to appreciate and enjoy it.
- Practice your survival skills on weekend/summer camping trips. Plan at least one snow camping trip and be prepared to survive in winter conditions, if you live in such an area. Disasters can happen any time of the year.
- Buy books on survival, farming, hunting, food processing, gardening and long-term survival. *READ THEM BEFORE YOU NEED THEM.*
- Make sure negatives of family photos, heirloom jewelry and important documents are in a bank safety deposit box.

4.**Preliminary Alert Status**: A situation you've noticed is capable of escalating into a problem down the road, but it's just a possibility right now. There is a typical rainstorm or snowstorm warnings on the news. Power may go out for a few hours or a week. Stay on your toes. Things you can do to be ready for this level:

- Check batteries in flashlights. Make sure that there is a source of light in every room of the house.
- Make sure you have enough water, toilet paper and hygiene supplies to last at least one week without dipping into your long-term storehouse supplies.

- Make sure you have enough fuel for a small camp stove. If you have an electric stove, make a few meals ahead of time that can be eaten cold, if necessary.
- Have a good supply of canned foods, meats and sandwich bread. Make a pot of coffee and pitchers of juice ahead of time.
- Make up pitchers of salted ice using cleaned milk jugs or two liters. They will help keep your freezer foods cold if the power goes out.
- Make sure all your dirty laundry is cleaned. Focus on towels, blankets, underwear and warm shirts. Have a bucket ready to wash clothes in as needed. Use spare sheets to cover windows and doors to help keep heat in.
- Have a bathroom bucket. You won't be able to flush the toilet. Use a bit of kitty liter to keep smells down.
- Have everyone take a shower before the power goes out. Being clean will help people from getting cranky. Be prepared to sponge bathe until the power comes back on.
- Have pens, paper, and card/board games ready to combat non-electronic boredom. Use the time to really talk to your kids about things they think about, find out what they are worried about, and talk about other survival situations.

3. **High Alert Status**: Cancel your plans for the weekend and gas up your vehicles. Things could get ugly REALLY fast. Flood, Earthquake or Hurricane warnings are on the news, and you may be advised to evacuate. Make sure your family understands that

this is NOT a time to argue or debate. This is not a drill – this is serious. You are in charge, and they can just deal with it until you are all somewhere safe. Connect with family or friends outside of the danger zone and make sure they are ready to have you stay with them. Hotels fill up fast. You can call around to churches in the area as well. Some are equipped to take people in and stay with members of the congregation. If all else fails, head to a campground with your gear. Stay frosty. You may not have a home to come back to, so be prepared to stay awhile until you can get back you're your feet. Things you can do to be ready for this level of emergency:

- Get your family all in one place and make sure everyone has his or her Bug Out Bag (BOB) ready. Gather the pets together in cages, or on leashes. Pets should have their own BOB with food bowls, water, food, treats, medications, pet brushes, etc.
- Have a destination in mind before you leave. Make sure your maps are easily accessible and you have extra gas cans ready to go.
- Go to the bank and get as much cash out as you can and your items in the safety deposit box. This should be the only stop you make. The longer you spend running around town getting ready to go, the harder it will be to leave the area. The supplies you have on hand are what you are taking. This is why we prepare in advance.
- If you have the time, make sure that your elderly neighbors have a place to go, and help them weatherproof their homes and put together a go bag if they don't have one. You may need to rely on

their kindness some day and a little effort on your part to make sure they are safe will be appreciated and remembered. Sometimes it's not just about you and yours.

2.**National or Local Emergency in Progress or Imminent**: You should be ready to go as soon as the evacuation is made mandatory, if not before hand. Take the back roads out of town, and head in the opposite direction as most of the people. You don't want to get stuck in a traffic jam. Get to where you need to be as fast as possible. Things you can do to be ready:

- Last minute checks on provisions, weapons, and family. Don't forget the pets.
- Vehicles are loaded and head to your escape locations BEFORE the highways get jammed. Take back roads.
- Bug Out Shelter or other family's home is ready for a long stay.
- Close and lock any perimeter enclosures and fencing.
- Unplug all electronics.
- Barricade windows, vents and sliding doors with plastic sheeting and sheets of plywood, as necessary.
- Take small family heirlooms and family photos with you, if you can. They can't be replaced.

1. **S has officially HTF**: This is the most major emergency you can think of. Loss or destruction of local or state infrastructure. Government is down and nobody is coming to help. Difficult to

travel due to traffic jams or damage. Ideally you want to already be out of dodge and somewhere safe ready to stay awhile. There is no telling when society will be up and running again. You are officially on your own. What you can do to be ready:

- Weapons should be loaded.
- No one goes anywhere alone.
- Listen to the radio for updates, if any.
- Hunker down and be prepared to stay a long while. Study the survival books for information related to your specific emergency situation.
- Start growing your heirloom seeds for food. They can be started indoors and transplanted outside later.
- Start collecting alternate sources of water.
- Begin hunting/fishing for alternate sources of meat. Build drying racks to smoke and dry meats for long-term storage.
- Have a daily routine. Each member of the family should have chores to do around the camp/shelter. No excuses. They depend on your efforts to survive, and you depend on theirs.
- Reinforce your camp/shelter for long-term defense and cold weather.

Chapter 2: The 72-Hour Pack or Bug Out Bag (BOB)

What is a Bug Out Bag and Why You Need One

A bug out bag is what will get you through the next 24-72 hours after an emergency or disaster. For example, if you are forced to evacuate from your home, you will want to be able to take some supplies with you, to get you by, until you can find someplace safe. Hopefully you'll never need it, but in the case of an emergency where you need to flee your home, car, or your city, packing essential safety and survival gear is the last thing on your mind but the most important. Disasters can happen at any time and it is best to be prepared.

Choosing the Right Bag

The average weight guidelines for a fully loaded backpack are no more than 25% of your overall body weight. For a 200-pound person (in good health), that would be 50 pounds for your BOB. You want to make sure most of whatever you put in your bag is as lightweight as possible. It's important to choose a bag that appropriately fits you, and has proper padding throughout the straps and hip area. A simple backpack isn't large enough for an adult bug out bag. You'll want a good-sized camp pack or hiking backpack, which distributes weight properly. Unless your bag is packed the right way, your center of balance will be off, making it hard for you to move quickly without injury.

Pack Smart – A bug out bag should be viewed as a life preserver in most situations, not a convenience store. Only take what is necessary to survive for 24-72 hours. Leave the rest.

What To Put in Your Bug Out Bag:

Below is a list of the absolute minimum requirements you and your family need to have with you in an emergency situation. In an adult BOB you need:

Water and Food
- A *minimum* of three liters of water. 1 per day, per person. More is better.
- Water purification tablets, canteen or water bladder system.
- A small cook stove and fuel.
- Waterproof matches, flint and tinder, a lighter. (One of them is necessary; all three is best)
- A mess kit that includes a cooking pot/large cup.
- A can opener.
- 9 'just add water meals', and high-energy granola or protein bars.
- Basic spices: Salt, Pepper, Garlic Powder, Chili Powder and Italian Seasoning make just about anything taste a little better. (Small amounts in waterproof containers.)

Shelter:
- A cold weather sleeping bag
- A tent or tarps. A family size tent is necessary for more than two people. A single person tent is barely big enough for one person, much less that person AND their gear. Two people need a 4-6 person tent. Anyone with kids or more than two people in their home need a family size tent or more than one 4-6 person tent.
- 1 sheet of large plastic. (Great for catching rainwater, or waterproofing your tent.)
- A silver reflective emergency blanket
- Use one of your tarps to cover over the roof of your tent. Use the second to cover your cooking area and a third to use to collect water. The fourth is a backup in case a hole gets in any of the others.

Clothing:
- A pair of water resistant boots that cover the ankle and have traction.
- A pair of long pants (preferably not blue jeans.)
- 2 Pairs of wool socks (not cotton), clean underwear.
- 2 Shirts (Maybe 1 long sleeve and 1 short sleeve for layering, not cotton.)
- A Jacket that is both warm and provides protection from rain (you'll be wearing it every day)
- A waterproof poncho
- Warm thermal underclothing.

- A winter hat, and gloves, if you live in a cold-winter area.
- A Bandana
- Dust mask and goggles

Other MUST Haves:

- Two sources of light. You should have at least one Maglight flashlight, and an LED lantern. Candles don't give off much light, and oil lamps can be dangerous if they topple over. Don't forget - Extra batteries.
- Camp saw to chop wood with.
- A personal defense weapon. A pistol is best – easier to store and carry than a rifle, powerful enough to do its job still.
- Plastic baggie full of: wash cloth, bar soap, mini toothpaste, and travel toothbrush, floss. Mini deodorant, shampoo and conditioner. Small hairbrush. Don't forget Toilet Paper!
- 2-3 plastic garbage bags.
- Emergency cash: $10 in quarters, $10 in ones, $10 in fives, $30 in tens, and $100 in twenties.
- An emergency whistle. Also, a Signal flair, Compass, and a Waterproof watch.
- A fold up map of the state you are in or the nearby area, at a minimum. (laminated).
- Emergency documents: birth certificates, social security card, passport, and emergency contact information.
- A Cold Steel Folding Camp Shovel and Survival Knife, or similar dual-purpose tool.

- 100 Feet of braided Paracord, Various sizes of zip ties.
- A first aid kit AND *Emergency War Surgery: The Survivalist's Medical Desk Reference* – quite literally, a life-saving book.
- An Altoids tin that has fishing line, hooks, sewing needles, and thread inside.
- A large roll of duct tape and two bottles of Gorilla Glue.
- Two way radio.

IF YOU HAVE ROOM FOR IT:
- Small copy of your chosen religious text.
- A deck of cards.
- Aqua shoes, so you don't cut your feet if you bathe in a water source. Protect those feet! (Shoes can dangle outside the bag so they don't take up room inside it.)

ESSENTIALS FOR BABIES:
- 4 Cloth diapers and safety pins, rash cream.
- 1-2 cans of formula (if you can't breastfeed).

If your baby has teeth, they are old enough to eat whatever you do. Just make sure it's cooked soft and in small portions.

- Baby carrier/sling
- Pacifier, teething toy
- Baby all in one Body Wash/Shampoo
- 2 Sleeper Feet Pajama outfits. (The really warm ones.)

- Baby mittens and socks. (2 pairs each.)

ESSENTIALS FOR CHILDREN 3+

Each child should have their own bug out bag. During a SHTF situation, it will be extremely important for your kids to feel as safe and secure as possible. Having their own child sized Bug Out Bag, filled with familiar items and comfort foods, can be a real lifesaver during an emergency. With children, comfort items often become a top priority to ensure their overall mental health during a SHTF scenario. Make sure they are lightweight and age appropriate. Heavier items and gear should be in the adults' bags.

Remember, a child's bug out bag is not meant to be an adult BOB. Its main purpose is to comfort your child during a stressful situation and give them a feeling of control. Make sure you customize the bag for your child's age, personality, and overall fitness level.

Suggested items can include:
- Emergency whistle, and a compass strapped to outside of bag so they can easily find it.
- Laminated emergency contact list with name, home address, and telephone numbers.
- Small soft fleece blanket
- 2 (non cotton) shirts, 1 pair of pants.
- Clean underwear, and extra sets (non-cotton socks)

- Coat, Rain gear and boots, hat and gloves
- Their own granola bars, water and juice mixes.
- Their own mini flashlight/lantern and batteries.
- Small first aid kit, toothpaste, toothbrush, bar of soap and Toilet Paper. Remember: It's good for you to have extras of the little stuff. These things are light enough for them to carry in the bottom of their bags.
- Dust mask and goggles
- Coloring book, crayons, stuffed animal, their favorite small book.

FOR OLDER CHILDREN (AGE 8+)

Their bag should be age appropriate but with several pockets to store things. A child of 8 or 9 years old should know how to build a simple fire to keep warm and boil water. If they get separated from you, they will need to have a way to stay warm and boil water to drink. *In addition* to the list above, have them also carry:

- A prepaid cell phone AND $10 in quarters.
- A decent pocket knife, and 100 feet of braided paracord.
- Flint and Tinder, Waterproof Matches
- Water purification tablets
- A deck of cards, 1 Battery operated game (yatzee, slingo etc.), a book.

CHIDLREN 12+

Teenagers are plenty old enough to know basic first aid, learn to build a fire and a simple lean to, memorize Morse code, navigate with a compass and know how to read a map. They should be able to cook a meal without burning it. Their packs should hold much of the same stuff yours does. They should have their own:

- Small tent, tarps, rope etc.
- Camp stoves/fuel, mess kits etc.
- First Aid Supplies, Boy Scout Survival Book etc.
- Tools, Knives, Paracord
- Many of the small items listed in the Adult BOB

These above lists are *not* everything you could ever need in a bug out bag, but they are a good start. Customize your bag for your environment and your family. You can take your BOB out camping a few times to help you decide what you need to keep and what you need to replace with better gear. The BOB will be your lifeline is a 24-72 hour survival situation, so it's vital to have one ready to go.

Chapter 3: Water

How much do you need?
You use a lot more water than you realize. Some people say you only need three liters of water a day, per person to survive. Yes, you can survive on that much water, but ideally, you need three *gallons* of water, per person, per day, to thrive instead of just survive. So, let's say your power is out for three days. 3x3=9 gallons of water for just one person. Multiply that number by however many people are in your family and that is how much water you need for 72 hours. That may seem like a lot, but let's break it down. You need at least 1 gallon per person to drink each day, 1 gallon per person to wash with, and 1 gallon to use for preparing three meals a day. One gallon could be used for washing wounds, giving to pets, soaking dehydrated foods, or cleaning dishes. The more water you have on hand, the less work you will have to do to replace what you use. Can you get by on less water? Yes, you can, but you don't want to have to. *When it comes to survival, one is none, and two is one.* That means: have duplicates of EVERYTHING. You want to have more than enough, especially when it comes to clean water.

Water Storage
Because of our modern conveniences of plastic bottles, water is easy to store. Water should be stored in a centrally located area, preferably close to the kitchen or outdoor cooking area. That's

where you will use a majority of it, and you don't want to have to haul water farther than you absolutely have to, not even through the house.

If you have the space in your pantry, line the bottom with gallon jugs of water. Better yet, clear out some space in a rarely accessed hall closet. You can turn it into an emergency pantry and store extra water, food stuffs, batteries, lanterns and medical supplies. You can easily stack cases of water against a wall, no more than five cases high (they could fall over). One 24 -pack of water bottles is roughly 3 gallons. No matter what you do, save your plastic bottles. They will come in handy for collecting more water down the line, or used for other things, like planting seeds in. Your BOB should have a water bladder system built into it, so that you can carry water on your back.

Finding Water
What do you do if you run out of water? The easiest thing would be to go buy more, but let me tell you something. Water will be the first thing to disappear from store shelves in an emergency situation. The best way to get clean water is to wait for it to rain and collect your rainwater. You can create a water drip system with a simple blue tarp, draining into a plastic food grade bucket. Be aware that if you choose to collect water this way, you'll want to be sure no one steals it before you've collected it. You'll want to guard your water source.

Another method of getting water requires a bit more effort. You'll have to find a natural water source and collect it from a stream. Water with a rushing current from a river is best, because it will be cleaner than stagnant, still water, say from a lake or pond. That means hauling water from that source. No matter how thirsty you are, you should never, I repeat NEVER, drink or bathe in water straight from a source without making sure it is as clean as you can get it. There is a lot of pollution and various water borne illnesses to consider.

Water Borne Illnesses

Water is the most important resource a person will need in order to survive after an emergency or disaster. The average person can survive for three to four days without water. Unfortunately, water from lakes and rivers often can be contaminated with chemicals or germs, which can cause serious illness or death. Most of the world's deadliest diseases are waterborne. Water can carry parasites, giardia, cryptosporidium, bacteria, algae, viruses and fungi. Diseases like dysentery, typhus and cholera all are spread by contaminated water and cause more human deaths than virtually any other cause.

Many serious infections can result from ingesting contaminated water. Cholera, tularemia, typhoid fever and shigellosis are only a few of the diseases you can be infected with in this manner. These diseases mainly infect the digestive tract, and symptoms vary in severity. The bodily fluids of an infected individual have contaminated water that others will use. Water diseases are more common in less-developed countries where sanitation is poor. If water lines are contaminated, it's not uncommon to see widespread infection. Many waterborne infections that are endemic to certain areas don't cause disease in local residents and are pathogenic only to visitors. Some of the most common waterborne illnesses are below, including:

Shigellosis is the most severe type of dysentery, which is an inflammatory infection of the bowels. It's caused by the Shigella dysentery bacterium, a pathogen that's particularly hazardous because it produces a powerful poison, known as Shiga toxin, that damages the intestines. Patients usually experience fever, abdominal pain and blood in their stools. According to the American Public Health Association, shigellosis is responsible for 600,000 deaths a year worldwide.

Typhoid fever is found worldwide. It's caused by the bacterium Salmonella typhi. Individuals become infected after coming into contact with food or water contaminated by an infected individual's feces or urine. Typhoid fever can be prevented with proper sanitation of water and food supplies, and effective vaccines for it have been developed. It also can be treated with a wide range of antibiotics, and it usually isn't fatal.

Cholera is a severe intestinal infection caused by the Vibrio cholerae bacterium. Symptoms are severe diarrhea and vomiting, which can quickly cause dehydration. If a water source is infected with this bacterium, a widespread outbreak will result. Cholera outbreaks have been reported worldwide, but now the disease is mainly confined to Africa, Asia and the Middle East.

Francisella tularensis is the cause of tularemia. Tularemia is a dangerous infectious disease that causes skin ulcers, swollen and painful lymph glands, chills and fatigue. Tularemia can be infect humans through arthropod bites as well as through the ingestion of contaminated water. Tularemia is treatable with antibiotics but can be fatal if left untreated.

Making Your Tap Water Safe to Drink

If you are on a treated municipal or public water system, occasionally these water plants can fail and contaminants can enter the water supply, or a natural disaster such as a flood, storm or earthquake can cause your water source to become contaminated and unsafe to drink. In these situations, your first priority is making tap water drinkable. Boiling water is often a temporary measure, until your local water authorities can restore the water quality of your drinking water. If your water is just a little bit cloudy, you can run it through a simple coffee filter to get out some of the sediments before you boil it. Your water should be boiled for at least 10 minutes and allowed to cool completely. This is generally the safest method to destroy any disease and organisms.

In order to boil water you will need a source of heat either from a fire or a camp/emergency stove and a camp pot or cup. To purify the water, bring it to a rolling boil for a *minimum* of 60 seconds plus one additional minute for each 1000 feet above sea level you are, in order to ensure that all living organisms are dead. If the water tastes flat after boiling, you may aerate it by pouring the water back and forth between two clean containers.

If it is still cloudy or smells off (don't taste it), you will have to use other methods of water purification before using the water. Water purification tablets are the most lightweight and portable solution. Two common types of tablets are available: Iodine and Chlorine Dioxide.

If possible, I recommend chlorine dioxide tablets. Like iodine, these are also a lightweight and portable solution for water purification. Chlorine Dioxide is a stronger pathogen killer than iodine and will not discolor the water. To use these tablets, drop them in your water and wait at least 15 minutes before drinking as per the instructions on the bottle. The water will have a slight chlorine taste. You also can use liquid bleach found in your home. Be sure the bleach you have on hand for this purpose contains only sodium hypochlorite (5.25% solution) with no soap, phosphates, scents, etc. For one gallon of clear water, add 8 drops (1/8 tsp) of bleach. To five gallons of clear water add 32 drops (1/2 tsp.) If the water is cloudy, double these amounts. Do not use the measuring dropper or spoon for anything else. At the time the bleach is purchased, write the date of purchase on the bottle. Bleach that is over one year old has lost about half its strength, so the quantities you use should be doubled. After adding the bleach to the water, mix well and let it stand for at least 30 minutes before using.

Iodine also has its advantages, however. Iodine will kill pathogens that are heat resistant. When using iodine, drop the tablet in the water and wait at least 30 minutes before drinking the water as per instructions on the bottle. You also can use liquid iodine. If there are no directions on the iodine bottle use 12 drops to the gallon of water. If the water is cloudy, double that quantity. Again, mix well and allow to stand for at least 30 minutes. Iodine is a quick and easy solution. Pregnant women and people who have thyroid problems should contact a physician before using iodine as a water purifier.

Both chlorine and iodine will impact the taste of the water. Pouring the water from one container to another several times will help dissipate some of that taste by re-oxygenating the water. Tang or Kool-Aid also will help to cover or disguise these tastes. Personally, I prefer using bleach to iodine, as it doesn't taste quite as bad.

Water Filters will remove bacteria and parasites. Filters also can remove many waterborne chemicals and filter out "off" tastes that boiling or tablets cannot. These filters are made in various sizes and output capacities. Some are small enough to be carried in a backpack. It would be advisable to have several of these on hand. Filters are an excellent option when you have the need for something that you can carry and that will last long term. As with all things, plan ahead and practice with the different tools and methods to find which one works best for you.

Chapter 4: Food

Next to water, food is the thing that most people will not think about stocking until it is too late. One thing to keep in mind about survival when it comes to food is that you will get very weak and malnourished without proper nutrition. In a survival situation, the food pyramid is almost completely backwards. You want extra carbohydrates and fats in your diet, to give you energy and keep you going. Surviving is stressful business, and stress will cause your body to crave instant energy. In everyday life, when we are sitting around in front of the computer or TV all day long, you don't use that extra energy and it gets stored as fat. It's okay to be on a low carb diet, because you don't *need* that extra energy.

This is not true in a survival situation, especially if you are on the move, in the wilderness and exercising more than you normally would in a day. Your body will burn through food faster and require more replacement energy: food. You need to realize that what you used to eat may not be what your body now requires and you will need to adjust your diet accordingly. Whatever special diet you are on now means nothing when it comes to survival. In a survival situation, being picky and deciding you aren't going to eat potatoes because they are too starchy is just plain stupid, and may even lead to your demise. When you are hungry enough, you'll eat whatever is available.

Another thing to consider is that when you are in a survival situation, and you are not used to going without electricity to entertain you, it is easy to get bored. Very bored. When we get bored, what do we want to do? Something, anything, and usually involving eating. Some people want to eat more when they are bored. You must resist this urge in order to conserve your food stores. When you are in survival mode, and lacking food stores, you MUST have water to drink. Your body requires extra water when you aren't eating properly.

Vitamins and Nutrition

The best way a person can prepare themselves for a survival situation is by adjusting their diet ahead of time. Quit smoking, drinking, and if you have an addiction to sugary desserts, energy drinks or coffee, it's time to cut it out of your diet before you are forced to. You don't want to have to deal with weird withdrawal symptoms while you are just trying to make it through the day in a survival situation. If you are used to eating chemical laden fast food burgers, pizza, burritos, chips, soda, candy, ding dongs etc., you are going to have a very hard time adjusting to eating the bare minimum nutritional requirements that you will find in a survival situation. For the most part, nothing that comes in a box, bag, or man-made package is healthy. Just because something is advertised as food, or advertised as healthy, doesn't mean you should be eating it. Most modern food is so full of chemicals that make us sick and drain our energy, it's amazing we are even still alive. The more processed a food is, the less amount of nutrients it will have in it by the time it reaches your body.

As a general rule, if your great-grandparents would not recognize it as food, you probably shouldn't be eating it. The closer you can eat to the garden, the healthier you will be. It's just common sense. People thousands of years ago didn't have Doritos or DQ, and they thrived. So can you. That means replacing your morning pop tart with oatmeal and fresh fruit. It means replacing your McDonalds French fries and burger with a hearty vegetable soup, a salad and whole wheat rolls. It means replacing your take out Chinese or pizza with fresh fish, rice and roasted summer vegetables. It means replacing your sugary soda with a bottle of water. The more you become accustomed to eating real foods, the less of a shock your body will go through in an emergency situation. Not only that, you'll be much healthier in the long run.

I suggest keeping a food diary of everything your family eats AND drinks for an entire month. You may be shocked. Figure out how much you rely on pre-packaged foods, processed sugars and convenient pre-made frozen dinners. You won't have any of those things to rely on when the SHTF and your body will attempt to reject real foods at first. The last thing you want in an emergency situation is a diarrhea problem to deal with. One of the best things you can do to prepare for a survival situation is get your family used to eating healthy, homemade non-processed foods.

Let's talk a little bit about vitamins. The more nutrients you put into your body through foods, the less supplements you will have to store or take. While a good multivitamin is important to give you a boost, you should not be relying on them to give you what you need. The better quality of food you eat, the healthier you are. The old saying is true: You are what you eat. In a life or death survival situation, the healthier you are, the better chances you will have to live.

You'll also want to start filling your food storage space or food storehouse. The cheapest way to create a food storehouse is to purchase a food dehydrator, vacuum bags and 5-gallon food storage containers. Commercially packaged freeze-dried and dehydrated foods are very expensive to stock up on enough for you or your family. You will end up spending thousands of dollars for a 45-day supply. Invest in the food dehydrator and a vacuum bag system to create your own stores. Most new dehydrators come with an instruction manual and easy to follow guidelines for how long to dry foods.

It is best to grow your own fruits and vegetables if you can, but if you live in the city and that isn't an option for you, then watch for store sales and stock up on fresh veggies and fruits. Farmers markets usually have cheaper produce than regular grocery stores, and the produce is usually much more nutritious for you. You can dehydrate half of it for your storehouse. Keep in mind that you will have to soak dehydrated food in water for several hours before you can eat it. That's what some of your extra water is for.

Here is a quick list of healthy foods you should start working on storing:

<u>FRUITS</u>
- Apples
- Apricots
- Banana
-Blackberry
- Blueberry
- Cherry
- Kiwi
- Lemon
- Mango
- Papaya
- Peaches
- Pears
- Pineapple
- Plums
- Pomegranate (Seeds)
- Strawberries

<u>VEGATABLES</u>

- Asparagus
- Beans
- Beets
- Broccoli
- Brussels sprouts
- Carrot
- Cauliflower
- Celery
- Collard Greens/ Swiss Chard/Kale
- Corn
- Cucumbers
- Leeks
- Mushrooms
- Onions
- Parsnips/Turnips
- Peas
- Peppers
- Pumpkins
- Radish
- Shallots
- Spinach
- Squash
- Tomatoes
- Yams
- Zucchini

CANNED FOODS:

- Nalley Chili (Can be eaten cold if you must.)
- Various Beans (You Should have Dried too.)
- Diced Tomatoes, Spaghetti Sauce, Tomato Paste
- Potatoes, Green Beans, Corn, Spinach Greens
- Mixed Veggies (Great for soups and stews.)
- Mixed Fruits, Applesauce, Peaches, Pears
- Tuna, Chicken or Ham
- Chocolate Sauce/ Baking Powders

OTHER FOOD THINGS TO STOCK UP ON IN THE HOME:

- Heirloom Seeds (To grow your own veggies and fruits if you must.)
- Peanuts, Almonds, Granola Bars
- Crisco, Vegetable and Olive Oil, Coconut Oil, White and Apple Cider Vinegar
- Pastas, Oatmeal, Pancake Mix, Dried Beans, Popcorn
- Grains: Quinoa, Wheat, Barley, Bulgur, Rye, Spelt, Rice, Millet
- Baking Soda, Baking Powder, Corn Starch, Cornmeal, YEAST
- Sugar, Brown Sugar, Honey
- Coffee, Powdered Milk, Hot Chocolate and Powdered Juice Mixes
- Egg Substitute, Powdered Cheese Substitute
- Chili, Taco, Meatloaf and Beef Stew, Ranch Packets (or make your own),
- Brown, White and Chicken Gravy

- Chicken, Beef and Vegetable Bullion Cubes
- Spices: Garlic, Onion, Cayenne, Pepper, Salt, Lemon Pepper, Cajun Spice, Italian Seasonings, Chili Powder, Dill, Cilantro, Chives, Cinnamon, Curry, Turmeric, Ginger, Nutmeg.
- Peanut Butter and Home Canned Jellies

WHAT *NOT* TO STOCK UP ON:

- Dairy Products, Butter, Eggs etc. (They don't keep well at all. Get powdered varieties of milk or butter, or learn to make it fresh yourself, if you must have it. Butter can be frozen, and last for some time out of the fridge, but eventually it will mold and go bad, just like everything else with dairy in it.)

- Frozen Meats (They will only last a day once they thaw, maybe two, if you're lucky. You can make beef jerky, or better yet, use canned meats like tuna, chicken and ham.)

- Ramen noodles (Great for a 72-hour pack, but surprisingly, doesn't hold flavor well after about three months. It also has NO real nutritional value, is loaded with sodium, and the makers *refuse* to say what chemicals they use to make the noodles shiny and not stick to each other. Not worth the risk for long-term food storage.)

- Canned Soups (Again, fine for a 72-hour pack, but they are heavy to carry, expensive to buy, and you can easily make a huge pot of soup for far cheaper than buying enough canned soup for every member of the house.)

- Boxed Instant Potatoes/Pastas/Bags of Flavored Rice (Don't last as long as you would think. They are okay for a 72-hour pack but they also require butter or milk to cook. If they get wet, the food is useless. They are processed foods full of chemicals with very little nutritional value.)

- Anything that requires refrigeration.

The more food you can successfully store before a crisis, the better. You may also need a method to move your food stores, if you can't stay where you are. That is why it is best to have lightweight, dehydrated foods. I suggest having two storage options for food preparation. Canned and store bought non-perishables can be stored in a closet for in home emergency use. You should also have a suitcase or two on wheels, full of food dehydrated and basic food-stuffs. This way, if you have to evacuate your home, you have a supply of food ready to take with you. There should also be a basic three-day supply in every 72-hour pack.

Chapter Five: Fire Building and Camp Living 101

Choosing a Campsite

If you are forced to camp out somewhere, there are a few things you will want to make sure your campsite has, including:

- A running water source, like a stream or river. Water with a current tends to be cleaner than standing water of a lake or pond.

- Flat ground area, preferably without rocks or major divets. Your camp should be on high ground, far enough away from the water source that you don't have to worry about flooding out your camp if it rains.

- Natural shelters are preferred, like caves, natural rock overhangs and abandoned cottages. Be sure they aren't inhabited.

- Your campground should be near enough trees to be able to have firewood readily available.

- If possible, look for naturally growing fruit bushes or trees. They may not be ripe now, but if you need to stay a while, you will have a natural food source.

- Overgrown tall grass can be cut and used as ground cover, and usually can be easily burned.

- Your campground should be easily defendable. Ideally, you want to limit the directions people can come in at, or at least make sure that you can clearly see anyone coming from any direction.

Types of Shelters

There are three major things you should be aware of when building a shelter.

1. How much time you have to build it. You don't want to get caught in the rain or snow. If you get too cold, you risk hypothermia. A quickly built shelter is better than none at all when bad whether strikes. You can always build a better shelter when the storm clears.

2. It should be built well enough to adequately protect you and your family from the elements (sun, rain, wind, snow)

3. It should be up big enough for the tallest person to stand up in and lay down comfortably, and wide enough for the tallest person to be able to spread their arms out and not touch the sides. *Note: Be sure not to make it too big.* A small shelter can be heated with your own body heat, and will help to prevent hypothermia during cold nights or in colder climates.

The following are different types of shelters, with some instructions on how to make each one, and tips for when they are best to use.

The Tarp Lean-To

It takes only a short time and minimal equipment to build this simple lean-to. You need a poncho, 2 to 3 meters of rope or parachute suspension line, three stakes about 30 centimeters long, and two trees or two poles 2 to 3 meters apart. Before selecting the trees you will use or the location of your poles, check the wind direction. Ensure that the back of your lean-to will be into the wind.

To make the lean-to:
- Tie off the hood of the poncho. Pull the drawstring tight, roll the hood the long ways, fold it into thirds, and tie it off with the drawstring.
- Cut the rope in half. On one long side of the poncho, tie half of the rope to the corner grommet. Tie the other half to the other corner grommet.
- Attach a drip stick (about a 10-centimeter stick) to each rope about 2.5 centimeters from the grommet. These drip sticks will keep rainwater from running down the ropes into the lean-to. Tying strings (about 10 centimeters long) to each grommet along the poncho's top edge will allow the water to run to and down the line without dripping into the shelter.

- Tie the ropes about waist high on the trees (uprights). Use a round turn and two half hitches with a quick-release knot.
- Spread the poncho and anchor it to the ground, putting sharpened sticks through the grommets and into the ground.

If you plan to use the lean-to for more than one night, or if you expect rain, make a center support for the lean-to. Make this support with a line. Attach one end of the line to the poncho hood and the other end to an overhanging branch. Make sure there is no slack in the line.

Another method is to place a stick upright under the center of the lean-to. This method, however, will restrict your space and movements in the shelter.

For additional protection from wind and rain, place some brush, your rucksack, or other equipment at the sides of the lean-to.

To reduce heat loss to the ground, place some type of insulating material, such as leaves or pine needles, inside your lean-to.

The Tarp Tent
This tent provides a low silhouette. It also protects you from the elements on two sides. It has, however, less usable space and observation area than a lean-to. To make this tent, you need a

poncho, two 1.5- to 2.5-meter ropes, six sharpened sticks about 30 centimeters long, and two trees 2 to 3 meters apart.

To make the tent:
- Tie off the poncho hood in the same way as the poncho lean-to.
- Tie a 1.5- to 2.5-meter rope to the center grommet on each side of the poncho.
- Tie the other ends of these ropes at about knee height to two trees 2 to 3 meters apart and stretch the poncho tight.
- Draw one side of the poncho tight and secure it to the ground pushing sharpened sticks through the grommets.
- Follow the same procedure on the other side.

If you need a center support, use the same methods as for the poncho lean-to. Another center support is an A-frame set outside but over the center of the tent. Use two 90- to 120-centimeter-long sticks, one with a forked end, to form the A-frame. Tie the hood's drawstring to the A-frame to support the center of the tent.

Field-Expedient Lean-To

If you are in a wooded area and have enough natural materials, you can make a field-expedient lean-to without the aid of tools or with only a knife. It takes longer to make this type of shelter than it does to make other types, but it will protect you better from the elements.

You will need two trees (or upright poles) about 2 meters apart; one pole about 2 meters long and 2.5 centimeters in diameter; five to eight poles about 3 meters long and 2.5 centimeters in diameter for beams; cord or vines for securing the horizontal support to the trees; and other poles, saplings, or vines to crisscross the beams.

To make this lean-to:
- Tie the 2-meter pole to the two trees at waist to chest height. This is the horizontal support. If a standing tree is not available, construct a biped using Y-shaped sticks or two tripods.
- Place one end of the beams (3-meter poles) on one side of the horizontal support. As with all lean-to type shelters, be sure to place the lean-to's backside into the wind.
- Crisscross saplings or vines on the beams.
- Cover the framework with brush, leaves, pine needles, or grass, starting at the bottom and working your way up like shingling.
- Place straw, leaves, pine needles, or grass inside the shelter for bedding.

In cold weather, add to your lean-to's comfort by building a fire reflector wall. Drive four 1.5-meter-long stakes into the ground to support the wall. Stack green logs on top of one another between the support stakes. Form two rows of stacked logs to create an inner space within the wall that you can fill with dirt. This action not only strengthens the wall but makes it more heat reflective.

Bind the top of the support stakes so that the green logs and dirt will stay in place.

With just a little more effort you can have a drying rack. Cut a few 2-centimeter-diameter poles (length depends on the distance between the lean-to's horizontal support and the top of the fire reflector wall). Lay one end of the poles on the lean-to support and the other end on top of the reflector wall. Place and tie into place smaller sticks across these poles. You now have a place to dry clothes, meat, or fish.

Swamp Bed

In a marsh or swamp, or any area with standing water or continually wet ground, this swamp bed keeps you out of the water. When selecting such a site, consider the weather, wind, tides, and available materials.

To make a swamp bed:
- Look for four trees clustered in a rectangle, or cut four poles (bamboo is ideal) and drive them firmly into the ground so they form a rectangle. They should be far enough apart and strong enough to support your height and weight, to include equipment.
- Cut two poles that span the width of the rectangle. They, too, must be strong enough to support your weight.

- Secure these two poles to the trees (or poles). Be sure they are high enough above the ground or water to allow for tides and high water.
- Cut additional poles that span the rectangle's length. Lay them across the two side poles, and secure them.
- Cover the top of the bed frame with broad leaves or grass to form a soft sleeping surface.
- Build a fire pad by laying clay, silt, or mud on one corner of the swamp bed and allow it to dry.

Another shelter designed to get you above and out of the water or wet ground uses the same rectangular configuration as the swamp bed. You very simply lay sticks and branches lengthwise on the inside of the trees (or poles) until there is enough material to raise the sleeping surface above the water level.

Debris Hut

For warmth and ease of construction, this shelter is one of the best. When shelter is essential to survival, build this shelter.

To make a debris hut:
- Build it by making a tripod with two short stakes and a long ridgepole or by placing one end of a long ridgepole on top of a sturdy base.
- Secure the ridgepole (pole running the length of the shelter) using the tripod method or by anchoring it to a tree at about waist height.

- Prop large sticks along both sides of the ridgepole to create a wedge-shaped ribbing effect. Ensure the ribbing is wide enough to accommodate your body and steep enough to shed moisture.
- Place finer sticks and brush crosswise on the ribbing. These form a latticework that will keep the insulating material (grass, pine needles, leaves) from falling through the ribbing into the sleeping area.
- Add light, dry, if possible, soft debris over the ribbing until the insulating material is at least 1 meter thick--the thicker the better.
- Place a 30-centimeter layer of insulating material inside the shelter.
- At the entrance, pile insulating material that you can drag to you once inside the shelter to close the entrance or build a door.
- As a final step in constructing this shelter, add shingling material or branches on top of the debris layer to prevent the insulating material from blowing away in a storm.

Tree-Pit Snow Shelter

If you are in a cold, snow-covered area where evergreen trees grow and you have a digging tool, you can make a tree-pit shelter.

To make this shelter:
- Find a tree with bushy branches that provides overhead cover.
- Dig out the snow around the tree trunk until you reach the depth and diameter you desire, or until you reach the ground.

- Pack the snow around the top and the inside of the hole to provide support.
- Find and cut other evergreen boughs. Place them over the top of the pit to give you additional overhead cover. Place evergreen boughs in the bottom of the pit for insulation.

Fire Building

This is another essential skill that you and your family will need to know in order to survive for any length of time.

Choosing a Spot: If you are in a wooded or brush-covered area, clear the brush and scrape the surface soil from the spot you have selected. Clear a circle at least 1 meter in diameter so there is little chance of the fire spreading.

If time allows, construct a fire-wall using logs or rocks. Be sure not to use wet rock because they can explode when heated. This wall will help to reflector direct the heat where you want it. It will also reduce flying sparks and cut down on the amount of wind blowing into the fire. However, you will need enough wind to keep the fire burning.

Sources of Tinder: You need a supply of small twigs, leaves or dry grasses to keep the initial spark burning. Before light the fire, have a supply of twigs, small kindling (on inch in diameter short sticks) and larger logs ready to burn. You don't want your little fire going out while you are running around collecting wood to keep it going.

- Birch bark
- Shredded paper or cardboard
- Steel wool
- Cattail fibers
- Gauze bandages
- Finely shredded plastic or rubber
- Punk wood
- Bird nests
- Tobacco (cigarettes or cigars—not chewing tobacco)
- Dandelion heads
- Sanitizing wipes
- Dry grass, pine needles, or leaves
- Lint
- Animal dung
- Seed down
- Sawdust
- Cotton balls, tampons, or maxi pads
- Plastic bags
- Cigarette filters
- Pine bark
- Hair or fur
- Bird down

- Diapers
- Rope, string or twine (natural or synthetic)
- Dead Spanish moss
- Nearly anything flammable, such as kindling sized sticks, once covered with petroleum jelly, shoe polish, Chap Stick, paraffin wax, lard, pinesap, or any accelerant like gasoline can be used as tinder as well.

Building the Fire

There are several methods for building a fire, each of which has advantages. The situation you find yourself in will determine which fire to use.

Tepee

To make this fire, arrange the tinder and a few sticks of kindling in the shape of a tepee or cone. Light the center. As the tepee burns, the outside logs will fall inward, feeding the fire. This type of fire burns well even with wet wood.

Lean-To

To lay this fire, push a green stick into the ground at a 30-degree angle. Point the end of the stick in the direction of the wind. Place some tinder deep under this lean-to stick. Lean pieces of kindling against the lean-to stick. Light the tinder. As the kindling catches fire from the tinder, add more kindling.

Cross-Ditch

To use this method, scratch a cross about 30 centimeters in size in the ground. Dig the cross 7.5 centimeters deep. Put a large wad of tinder in the middle of the cross. Build a kindling pyramid above the tinder. The shallow ditch allows air to sweep under the tinder to provide a draft.

Pyramid

To lay this fire, place two small logs or branches parallel on the ground. Place a solid layer of small logs across the parallel logs. Add three or four more layers of logs or branches, each layer smaller than and at a right angle to the layer below it. Make a starter fire on top of the pyramid. As the starter fire burns, it will ignite the logs below it. This gives you a fire that burns downward, requiring no attention during the night.

How to Make a Stone Oven to Cook With

YOU WILL NEED:

A small shovel

Gloves

A strong back and arms

Plenty of stones

At least two large flat stones at least 3-4 inches thick

BASIC CONSTRUCTION:

Step 1: Choose a safe location for a fire, away from trees and plants. Brush away any leaves, pine needles, or any other loose forest debris that may catch fire.

Step 2: Dig a small hole approximately one foot in diameter and about six inches deep. Save this soil off to the side, not far from your fire, for extinguishing your fire when needed.

Step 3: Collect stones of all sizes and bring them to your stone oven location. Avoid gathering stones from a river or any source of water because they may crack or explode after they heat up.

Step 4: Begin laying medium to large size stones in a half circle shape. You'll need to wrap the stones around to make a shape of a semi-circle. Shape your stone oven to have an opening large enough for you to be able to reach into with your bread but not so large an opening that your oven does not stay consistently hot. I measure about two hand lengths for my stone oven opening.

Step 5: When you have stacked stones about two hand lengths high, place the flattest stone (large) on top. Your side walls need to be thick enough to support this large flat stone and another that will go on top. Make adjustments as you go.

Step 6: Continue stacking small to medium stones to build a higher stone oven wall. You are now building the height of the area you will bake in.

Step 7: Place your second large flat stone on top. This is your final and highest layer. Check to see that your oven space is high enough inside. If it is not, remove the large flat stone and build up your oven walls some more and try again.

Step 8: Fill any large holes in your stone oven by filling with small stones.

Step 9: Dig a small (very small) trench in the back of the stone oven so that air and smoke circulates.

Step 10: Build a small fire where you dug out the hole (underneath the bottom large flat stone) and give the stones time to heat up. Place your biscuits or flat bread on the stone inside and bake.

Some Additional Tips for Harmonious Camp Living

The best way to keep camp life peaceful is to make sure everyone knows the rules. For example:

- No one sleeps in. The first person to wake, wakes everyone else up. No one gets to be lazy. If you don't work, you don't eat.
- Everyone has a job to do to keep the fire going, gather firewood, gather water, preparing food, washing dishes etc.
- Don't sneak food or waste water.
- Keep the camp clean.

Other things to keep in mind:
- You should always have a pot of water boiling, for drinking, cooking or washing.
- If you have enough people in your group, make sure to take turns staying up to keep the fire going.
- No one should go anywhere alone. There is safety in numbers.

Chapter Six: First Aid

The First Aid Kit

This is the basic supply you want to have. It is a good idea for every adult to have a first aid kit in his or her 72-hour pack. Also, you can put one in your gym bag, in your car and in your area at work. It should include:

- 2 absorbent compress dressings (5 x 9 inches)
- 25 adhesive bandages (assorted sizes)
- 1 adhesive cloth tape (10 yards x 1 inch)
- 5 antibiotic ointment packets (approximately 1 gram)
- 5 antiseptic wipe packets.
- Small bottle of iodine or rubbing alcohol.
- 2 packets of aspirin (81 mg each)
- 1 emergency blanket (Now you have two.)
- 1 breathing barrier (with one-way valve)
- 1 Finger splint
- 1 instant cold compress
- 2 pair of no latex gloves (size: large)
- 2 hydrocortisone ointment packets (approximately 1 gram each)
- 1 roller bandage (3 inches wide)
- 1 roller bandage (4 inches wide)
- 5 sterile gauze pads (3 x 3 inches)
- 5 sterile gauze pads (4 x 4 inches)
- Oral thermometer (non-mercury/no glass)

- 2 triangular bandages
- Sterile plastic tubing
- Sterile needles, strong thread
- Tweezers and surgical scissors.
- Snake bite and bee sting kits
- Any prescription medications
- Travel size: Benadryl, Bayer Aspirin, aloe vera, sunscreen, hand sanitizer.
- Small box of tampons, sanitary napkins
- First aid instruction booklet

The First Aid Basics

CPR

There is no substitute for proper training. However, emergencies wait for no one. Every member of your family should be properly trained in CPR. Even children can learn it.

Infants (Under 1 Year of Age)

1. Try to wake the baby. Really small babies respond well to having the soles of their feet rubbed or tapped. For infants more than 2 months old, tap their shoulder or chest. In either case, call out his name in a loud voice. Don't hurt the baby but be aggressive; you're trying to wake him up. If someone is with you, have them call 911, if possible.

2. Check to see if they are breathing. If they aren't (or you aren't sure) go to step three.

3. Begin chest compressions Put two fingers on the breastbone directly between the baby's nipples. Push straight down about an inch and a half -- or about a third of the thickness of the baby's chest -- and then let the chest all the way back up. Do that 30 times, about twice per second.

4. Give the baby two breaths After pushing on the chest 30 times, cover the baby's entire mouth and nose with your mouth and *gently* blow until you see his or her chest rise - (chest, *not* their stomach). Let the air escape -- the chest will go back down -- and give one more breath. If no air goes in when you try to blow, adjust the baby's head (tilt the head back, allowing the throat to be exposed) and try again. If that doesn't work, then skip it and go back to chest compressions (step 3), you can try rescue breaths again after 30 more compressions.

5. Keep doing CPR and call 911 after 2 minutes If you are by yourself, keep doing CPR for 2 minutes (about 5 groups of compressions) before calling 911. If someone else is there or comes along as you are doing CPR, have that person call 911. Even if the baby wakes up, you need to call 911 any time you had to do CPR. Once 911 has been called or you have someone else calling, keep doing CPR. Don't stop until help arrives or the baby wakes up.

Children (1-8 Years Old)

1. Attempt to wake the child.

2. Lock your fingers together and place hands directly between the child's nipples to begin compressions. Compressions should be two inches deep.

3. When giving the breaths, tilt the head back-lifting the chin, cover the child's mouth and pinch the nose closed. Give two gentle breaths. Watch to see if the chest rises and falls, then give another breath.

4. If they do not start breathing, repeat compressions and breathing until they do. If the victim is breathing, briskly rub your knuckles against the victim's sternum until they regain consciousness.

CPR for Adults (8 Years and Older)

1. Attempt to wake victim. If the victim is not breathing call 911 immediately and go to step 2. If someone else is there to help, one of you call 911 while the other moves on to step 2.

2. Begin chest compressions. If the victim is not breathing, place the heel of your hand in the middle of his chest. Put your other hand on top of the first with your fingers interlaced. Compress the chest at least 2 inches (4-5 cm). Allow the chest to completely recoil before the next compression. Compress the chest at a rate of at least 100 pushes per minute. Perform 30 compressions at this rate (should take you about 18 seconds).

3. It's normal to feel pops and snaps when you first begin chest compressions - DON'T STOP! You're not going to make the victim worse. Getting them breathing is the most important thing.

4. Begin rescue breathing. After 30 compressions, open the victim's airway using the head-tilt, chin-lift method. Pinch the victim's nose and make a seal over the victim's mouth with yours. Use a CPR mask if available. Give the victim a breath big enough to make the chest rise. Let the chest fall, then repeat the rescue breath once more. If the chest doesn't rise on the first breath, reposition the head and try again.

5. After 2 minutes of chest compressions and rescue breaths, stop compressions and recheck victim for breathing. If the victim is still not breathing, continue CPR starting with chest compressions.

6. Repeat the process, checking for breathing every 2 minutes (5 cycles or so), until help arrives. If the victim wakes up, you can stop CPR.

Preventing and Treating Hypothermia

Hypothermia ranges from mild chills and shivering to coma and death. Hypothermia is defined as a core body temperature of less than 95 degrees Fahrenheit. Hypothermia signs and symptoms include:

- shivering
- exhaustion

- confusion
- slurred speech
- memory loss
- fatigue
- loss of motor control (fumbling hands)

Some cold exposures are worse than others. Wet victims lose body heat much faster than dry victims. Windy conditions cause victims to lose heat very quickly as well. Know your environment and you'll be better able to treat hypothermia.

Steps to treat hypothermia:
1. Make sure the victim has an airway and is breathing.
2. *Stop the exposure.* Move the victim to warm, dry shelter.
3. Remove wet clothing - leave dry clothing on victim.
4. Wrap the victim with blankets. Warming blankets (like electric blankets) work the best.
5. Chemical heat packs can be used on the victim's groin, neck, and armpits.
6. Victims that are able to follow commands and sit upright may drink warm, non-alcoholic beverages.

You should know:
As hypothermia progresses, shivering stops in order for the body to conserve energy. A victim of hypothermia that has stopped

shivering may be getting worse rather than better. Victims of cold exposure may also be suffering from frostbite.

Alcohol may feel like it warms the body, but that's because it flushes the skin with warm blood. Once the blood is at the surface of the skin, it is easily cooled. Alcohol speeds hypothermia. It can also cause dehydration.

As severely hypothermic victims begin to recover, cold blood from the extremities is pulled back to the core of the body. This can lead to a decrease in core body temperature and worsens the hypothermia. Watch hypothermia victims closely. They may suffer sudden cardiac arrest and require CPR.

Stopping Bleeding

Regardless how severe it may be, all bleeding can be controlled. If left uncontrolled, bleeding may lead to shock or even death. Most bleeding can be stopped before the ambulance arrives at the scene. While you're performing the steps for controlling bleeding, you should also be calling for an ambulance to respond. Bleeding control is only part of the equation.

The first step in controlling a bleeding wound is to plug the hole. Blood needs to clot in order to start the healing process and stop the bleeding. Just like ice won't form on the rapids of a river, blood will not coagulate when it's flowing.

The best way to stop it is to...stop it. Put pressure directly on the wound. If you have some type of gauze, use it. Gauze pads hold the blood on the wound and help the components of the blood to stick together, promoting clotting. If you don't have gauze, terrycloth towels work almost as well.

If the gauze or towel soaks through with blood, add another layer. *Never* take off the gauze. Peeling blood soaked gauze off a wound removes vital clotting agents and encourages bleeding to resume.

If the bleeding is more severe, spurting or doesn't stop after a few minutes, consult the Emergency War Surgery Guide in the Survivor Family Library for continued steps to stop bleeding.

Treating Shock

Shock is essentially a decrease in blood flow to the brain and other important organs.

1. Make sure the victim is breathing. If not, begin CPR
2. Before any other treatments for shock are done, bleeding must be stopped.
3. If you do not suspect a neck injury, lay the victim on his or her back (supine) and elevate the legs. As a general rule, if the victim is pale faced, raise the legs above heart level. If the victim is red, raise the head.

If you suspect a neck injury, do not move the victim. Car and other vehicle accidents often lead to neck injuries. Neck injuries are also common in falls, especially falls from a height taller than the victim.

1. Keep the victim warm. Cover them with blankets and talk reassuringly to them. If they are conscious, try to keep them conscious. Try to get them to respond to you. If they do not, note how long it takes them to respond, or how long it has been since they have been unresponsive.

2. Continue to check on the victim. If the victim stops breathing, begin rescue breathing. If the victim vomits, roll the victim to one side and sweep the vomit from his or her mouth with your fingers.

Treating Heat Stroke

Heat stroke occurs when heat exhaustion is left untreated and the victim's core body temperature continues to rise. Heat stroke is a severe emergency that can lead to coma, irreversible brain damage and death. Learn to recognize heat stroke and treat the victim aggressively to prevent further injury.

- Signs and symptoms of heat stroke:
- Coma or confusion.
- Hot, flushed, dry skin
- Red, Swollen fingers, throbbing of heartbeat in fingers.
- Deep, rapid breathing sometimes sounds wheezy.
- Possibly Seizures.

Steps to treat Heat Stroke:

1. Assure that the victim has an airway and is breathing.
2. Move the victim to a cooler environment immediately. Shade is better than sun; air conditioning is better than outside, etc. The cooler, the better.
3. Remove the victim's clothing to encourage heat loss.
4. Put ice on the armpits, groin, and neck area. Cool the victim as aggressively as possible.
5. Strip the victim completely to facilitate cooling.
6. Cover the victim with a sheet soaked with water to cool the victim's body.
7. Use ice at the victim's armpits, neck, and groin.
8. DO NOT give the victim of heatstroke anything to drink.

Index

The Surviving Family Library: 10 Essential Books

1. Hawke's Green Beret Survival Manual
2. Emergency War Surgery: The Survivalist's Medical Desk Reference
3. Dressing & Cooking Wild Game: From Field to Table: Big Game, Small Game, Upland Birds & Waterfowl (The Complete Hunter)
4. Country Wisdom & Know-How: A Practical Guide to Living off the Land
5. The Dehydrator Bible: Includes over 400 Recipes
6. Homegrown Herbs: A Complete Guide to Growing, Using, and Enjoying More than 100 Herbs
7. Economic Food Storage Strategies for Disaster Survival: Start Today and Have Enough Food Your Family Will Eat to Survive Any Disaster without Going Broke
8. Field Guide to North American Edible Wild Plants
9. Prepper's Long-Term Survival Guide: Food, Shelter, Security, Off-the-Grid Power and More Life-Saving Strategies for Self-Sufficient Living
10. Cook Wild: Year-Round Cooking on an Open Fire

BASIC COMMUNICATION

MORSE CODE

Morse code is an alphabetic code of long and short sounds. Each letter in the alphabet has a corresponding sound or series of sounds unique to it. The long sounds are referred to as *dashes*, while the short sounds are *dots*. Varying lengths of silence denote spaces between letters or words.

American Samuel Finely Breese Morse (1791-1872) invented the telegraph and this code in 1836. It was successfully tested on 24 May 1844, when Morse himself sent the first message between Washington DC and Baltimore.

The most well known Morse code phrase is **SOS** (save our souls). SOS was chosen because the code for it — three dots followed by three dashes followed by three dots — is unmistakable as anything else and recognizable even to those who do not know the code, and is important for everyone to know, in case of emergency.

A .-	N -.	0 -----
B -...	O ---	1 .----
C -.-.	P .--.	2 ..---
D -..	Q --.-	3 ...--
E .	R .-.	4 ....-
F ..-.	S ...	5 .....
G --.	T -	6 -....
H	U ..-	7 --...
I ..	V ...-	8 ---..
J .---	W .--	9 ----.
K -.-	X -..-	Full stop
L .-..	Y -.--	.-.-.-

M --	Z --..	Comma --..--

THE MILITARY ALPHABET

ALPHA
BETA
CHARLIE
DELTA
ECHO
FOXTROT
GOLF
HOTEL
INDIA
JULIET
KILO
LIMA
MIKE
NOVEMBER
OCTOBER
PAPA
QUEBEC
ROMEO
SIERRA
TANGO
UNIFORM
VICTOR
WHISKEY
X-RAY

YANKEE

ZULU

Prepper's Pantry: A Food Survival Guide

Introduction

Preparing for a sudden economic downturn is something that has gotten a lot of mainstream media attention in the last few years. With the popularity of the television show "Doomsday Preppers," people who were not at all involved in the "prepper" lifestyle are suddenly interested in developing a stockpile of necessities for that "just in case" day that preppers talk about.

What is a "prepper"? Simply put, it's one who prepares for the possibility that the world may catastrophically change at some point in our future, leaving food supplies, fuel supplies, and our current lifestyles drastically changed. Those reasons for change could be local, regional, or even on a worldwide scale.

Before the availability of long distance trucking, and even international shipping, of fresh meats and produce, most people "prepped," to some degree. Most likely, your grandparents had a garden, and canned or otherwise preserved the food they grew and harvested throughout the summer, so that they would have food for the coming winter. They may have even had a cow and a pig or two, and butchered regularly, either freezing or canning the meat to add to their winter stores. If you read the "Little House On The Prairie" books when you were younger, you were introduced to the prepper lifestyle; in those days, preparing for the winter was a matter of necessity. Without the proper supplies in place, families would die of starvation.

Modern supermarkets have made the need to do this kind of yearly prepping all but disappear. Almost any type of fruit or vegetable is available year round, if you're willing to either pay a high enough price for it, or buy it already canned or frozen. Modern meat packing plants butcher cows and pigs daily, with the animals being brought to feedlots a few weeks before slaughter, to pack on pounds and insure that you can buy bacon whenever you're in the mood for it. Modern food preservation methods mean that food can sit on store and home shelves for months, even years, without going bad. Truthfully, it's easier, and often cheaper, to buy your produce already canned, than it is to grow a garden and preserve it yourself. So much easier, in fact, that home food preservation is rapidly becoming a lost art.

Many people with the prepper mindset have developed a balance between preserving fresh food at home, and the use of supermarkets or wholesale clubs to enhance their personal stores. The methods of preparing that work best for you will depend on many factors such as your budget, the availability of certain tools and kitchen appliances, space, and your personal reasons for prepping.

Preppers stockpile food for a variety of reasons. Some people, much like our grandparents, stockpile food because their work is seasonal. Maybe the primary wage earner is a construction worker, who doesn't work much in the winter. Some people prepare because they are contract employees, and they know that they may not have a contract at any given point. Having three or six months' worth of food on hand is one less expense they will have to worry about while job hunting. They may be preparing for an economic downturn, or simply taking advantage of sale prices. Finally, they may be preparing for TEOTWAWKI, or The End Of The World As We Know It.

The TEOTWAWKI scenario is one that has been gaining ground in recent years. There are many reasons people think that humanity will undergo a catastrophic change in the coming years. Peak oil, the theory that we have drilled the most oil we will ever get, and that available supplies will slowly dwindle to extinction, is an often-cited fear. Climate change or catastrophic weather event are also near the top of the list of reasons why people prep. There are people afraid of a shadow government or New World Order, and there are some people concerned about a biblical Armageddon.

The reasons why you prep really don't matter. What matters is how long you're prepping for, and the means you go about doing it. This guide will show you how to determine your food needs, no matter how long you will be prepping for, and will discuss various methods of obtaining and storing food stockpiles.

Chapter One: Determining Your Food Preparation Needs

Determining your food preparation needs can be dependent upon many factors. The two most important factors are length of time you're preparing for, and how many people you will need to feed with the food that you stockpile. People prepping for seasonal job loss may be prepping for three or six months. A "Doomsday Prepper" may be prepping for years.

Another major determining factor in building your food stockpile is space. You need to determine if you've got enough protected storage space for the food that you want and need to store. This storage space can be inside your house, in your garage, or in secure outbuildings. Make sure you can protect your food storage from animals of all types, and from wet, freezing, or humid conditions. Below are different suggestions for storage

Glass – Ideal for most foods, glass can take the form of jars of water bath or pressure canned foods, vacuum-sealed storage containers, or containers with screwed on lids. Glass also works very well for freezing soups, broths, and foods not appropriate for canning, if you have the space in your freezer. Cost can be considerable. A water bath canner can run you $40-$60, and canning jars can cost up to $10/dozen if bought new. The explosion in popularity of Mason jar crafts has made it difficult to find used canning jars for a reasonable price. However, if you take careful care of your jars, you won't need to buy many more with subsequent canning seasons. Expect to pay between $100 and $200 for a good quality pressure canner. Glass does a good job of keeping out smaller pests like bugs and mice, but the breakable jars can result in food loss if they are knocked over.

Plastic jars – The great thing about plastic jars is that they can usually be found or scrounged for free. The peanut butter and mayonnaise that you're probably already buying comes in them, and your friends, family and neighbors may be willing to save their own for you. Craigslist or freecycle are also great sources. Plastic jars can hold dehydrated foods as long as you're storing them in dark pantries or cabinets. They're also good for longer-term storage of dried herbs and spices. Generally, you can also use them for freezing, too. Try to find BPA free plastic. The cost here is minimal, since you're mainly going to be using jars you already own. Plastic storage systems can be purchased, but avoid those with square tops, and those that can be purchased at dollar stores, if you want to use them for freezing. Plastic jars will keep out bugs, but not mice. If you only use these jars for freezing, then you will have less overall food loss.

Plastic bags – While these aren't great for long-term storage (unless you're also going to be putting the filled plastic bags into larger hard plastic containers), they are just fine for short-term storage, and the freezer bags are fine for freezing smaller cuts of meat. Just don't thaw in the microwave or reheat inside the bags.

Just a few dollars a week will keep you supplied with plastic bags. If you're storing in plastic bags, it's a good idea to rotate your food stock into fresh bags every six months or so. Plastic breaks down over time, giving your food items less protection.

Vacuum bags – Vacuum systems are ideal for long-term storage of many items. They are great for long-term storage of dehydrated foods, and keep any frozen food fresher, for longer. Vacuum storage also works well for matches, first aid kits, and paper goods for your bug out bags, as the vacuum bags will keep them dry while they sit in storage waiting to be used, or if you need to bug out in the rain. A vacuum system can cost up to $200, and the bags aren't very cheap either, but used efficiently, they are definitely worth the financial investment.

Most households will find themselves using a combination of these methods, depending on the types and sources of foods they are stockpiling. In addition to the costs above, if you're thinking of purchasing a dehydrator, you can get a basic one for around $50, at your local discount store or online, while the top of the line Excalibur dehydrator is about $300. If you're going to have a garden and dry your own produce from there, the Excalibur is definitely a better choice. If you are looking to make the best use of sale prices or warehouse club stock-ups, then you can go with a smaller model. Dehydrating and canning are both time consuming, and can be fairly labor intensive, but in terms of ability to preserve the most food, and keeping your own personal costs down while retaining the best quality possible, these are definitely the methods to go for.

Both dehydrating and canning also offer the added bonus of being able to put together "convenience foods." These meals are often cooked in one pot, and cook up fairly quickly, so you don't have to be busy in the kitchen for hours. This is an important consideration if both parents work, or if, during a TEOTWAWKI situation, both adults would need to be engaged in manual labor that would take them out of the kitchen. By the time you come in from what you're doing, you're tired and hungry, and the less you have to wait for food to cook, the better. Dehydrated meals often take less time to reheat, but they are better than nothing.

Now that you've been introduced to basic methods of food preservation, it's time to figure out how to determine your household's needs for a specific time frame. Keeping these methods in mind, you'll need to determine how much storage space that you have. For a family of two, a set of shelves stashed in a corner and a bit of freezer space could easily store three months worth of food. A family of six that wants to stockpile a years' worth of food is going to need much more room.

There is no hard and fast formula for determining how much space your stockpile will take up. That's dependent upon many factors.

For example, dehydrated carrots take up much less space than canned carrots. However, if you're storing primarily dehydrated food, you'll need to store more water than the basic recommendations of one gallon per person, per day, or have access to a clean, steady water supply. If you're storing canned carrots, you can use the packaging fluid, which is mostly water, as a base for cooking rice, potatoes, or re-hydrating some other type of dried food.

You also want to make sure that your stockpile contains food that can actually be made into meals. It's great to have several flats of vegetables, cases of pasta and 18 gallons of water. But without some type of sauce or seasoning, you may not be very happy with your food choices. Children certainly wouldn't want to eat the meal you could come up with, with those ingredients.

So as you're building your stockpile, you'll need to actually plan what meals you can make with those ingredients, and how you can best preserve or obtain the foods needed to fill in the holes on your meal plan. If you're doing any of your prepping by buying items on sale at your grocery store, it can be particularly easy to fall into this trap. But if you think creatively and out of the box, you can make more healthy, structured meals that will feed your family.

If you're looking at this week's store sale ad and you notice that green chiles are on sale, then you can buy a bushel of roasted green chiles, and make green chili to be canned. For that you'll need pork, some chicken broth, and perhaps some tomatoes. Well, last week, chicken was on sale, so if you stocked up on that, you have plenty available to put into a pot and make broth with, also yielding you several pounds of cooked chicken for additional meals. Also in this week's sale ad are pork ribs. While ribs aren't the traditional cut that green chili is made with, there's no rule that says you can't use them. That green chili will make an excellent topping for burritos or is great in a bowl by itself.

So here's what you have determined from looking at this week's sale ad:
- Green chiles are on sale, so green chili can be made and canned
- Pork Ribs are on sale, so they can be the meat in the green chili
- Pork Ribs are on sale, so canning some meat from them will yield some very tender pork that could be added to BBQ sauce and served on sandwiches or over mashed potatoes
- Chickens were on sale last week, so chicken broth can be made. The resulting chicken meat can be frozen and used for casseroles or as filling for the burritos that the green chili will smother.

For the burritos, you'll also need to buy beans, and the ingredients to make tortillas (flour, baking soda, lard, salt), and, if you're sure you'll have power to keep your freezer running during whatever event you're stockpiling for, some cheese to go on the burritos.

Add some rice and vegetables to the smothered burritos and you've got a great meal.

So with the purchase of a bushel of green chiles and several pounds of pork ribs and chicken, you've already got some key ingredients for several meals. Now that you've made some initial plans, you can sit down and do some planning.

As you're planning your stockpile, the most important factor to keep in mind is food fatigue. Using the scenario above, you could make enough green chili to feed your family for several days. But if you've ever given the side eye to the turkey that's been the mainstay of every meal for the last four days after Thanksgiving, you can understand the issue of food fatigue. This becomes even more critical in TEOTWAWKI situations because people are often performing tasks they are unfamiliar with, and doing more manual labor than they were used to, and every single calorie that is consumed is important, because each calorie is being used, rather than sitting there doing nothing but becoming fat. If you are sick of the food that's being served to you, you won't eat it. Your body won't let you. It's not a matter of convincing yourself that you need to eat. Your body will trigger responses such as nausea that will prevent you from being able to eat the food, and you will go without those much-needed calories. It's extremely important that you plan to have as wide a variety as possible of food available for your family in these extreme situations.

It's a good idea to build your stockpile a week at a time. This way, crucial ingredients aren't lost in the shuffle. You keep your mind on your purpose and can make sure that things are done efficiently. It may take you three or four weeks' worth of shopping to build a week's worth of stockpile, if you are doing most of your stockpiling from the grocery or warehouse store. If you are doing part of your stockpile from a garden or from butchering your own meat, planning this way still gives you a good idea of what you do need to buy at the store, so that you can fill in any holes as certain foods go on sale.

As you can see, just from this week's sale ad, you've got two meals planned, with notes about what you still need to obtain. Because you're familiar with different types of food preservation methods, you can note what methods you want to use for different items. How much of these items to buy and keep stocked, or preserved, will be determined from this list.

It's important to note that by using a list like this, you're giving yourself ideas. Things may happen that prevent you from using the list in its entirety. But a list like this is a starting point-somewhere for you to start making your plans. You can make other tables like the one above for different weeks. Look at how many quarts or pints of green chili you got canned, determine how many you want to keep for non stockpile use, and then go through your stockpile meal plans and add in either smothered burritos or a bowl of green chili every few weeks until you would have gone through the stock that you made.

To fill in the rest of the meal plan, you'll want to determine your garden plans, if you have space and time to garden, and look at the sale ads and determine what would be cheaper to buy at the warehouse store, if you have space. So maybe next week you add a spaghetti dinner, because pasta and sauce are on sale. If you can afford to, buy enough pasta and sauce for several weeks, and fill in those weeks as you need them. Remember that when you bought beans for the burritos, you bought a large bag. You can plan a meal with beans and canned ham, or use beans as a side to a chicken casserole. Try to find and print new recipes to add to the versatility of the foods that you are stockpiling.

Above all, and especially if you have children, buy food that you are familiar with. If your goal is to supplement your food stores with items like rice and beans, that store well for years, make sure that you introduce these foods to your family before they become a necessity. It's great to have 12 quarts of green chili ready to go in an emergency, but if your kids have never eaten it, you may find mealtime to be a battle, and that's one thing you won't have time for if you're in a TEOTWAWKI situation! If you're relying on either home-canned or store bought canned meats to be an important part of your stockpile, make a meal with these once a month or more, so that your family can get used to the texture and flavor of these foods. The same goes with any foods that you are planning on using in a different form than you usually do. Canned spinach tastes vastly different than fresh, which tastes vastly different than frozen.

As you're making your plans, take special note of quantities. If there's only one or two in your household, then you don't need to plan meals that will feed six, unless you're planning on inviting people with marketable skills to join you and create a compound of sorts for a TEOTWAWKI situation. But also remember that you may need more calories in that type of situation. Further, we tend to want to consume more calories in winter than summer, and if you will no longer have access to a gym or somewhere out of the elements to work out, that could be an issue, if you're not the one doing manual labor. Also remember that a pound of dehydrated food does not equal a pound of fresh, and that a pint of soup is pretty close to the condensed soups that you see in the store, but that you won't need to add water.

You should also remember that if you are in a TEOTWAWKI situation, your very survival depends on the quality of the food you are consuming. This is where you need to balance the so very important need to buy food that you are familiar with, and the need to make sure that each calorie you consume is one that your body can use as fuel. In other words, don't plan boxed macaroni and cheese too often, even though your kids love it and it's something you're certain they will eat. Make sure that they are getting plenty of fruits, vegetables, and whole grains now so they are used to it when they are essential. If you're going to be hunting for your meat, make sure everyone in your family knows what venison and wild game tastes like so they aren't surprised when that may be the only protein you have access to. Make whole grain breads part of your meal plans now, so that when you're relying on them to fill hungry bellies, the kids will enjoy their flavor and texture rather than find them new and intimidating.

This is why, what you're preparing for is of huge importance for what you prep. While it should always be a goal to serve the healthiest meals possible, boxed macaroni and cheese is quick and easy for many families and its okay to indulge once in awhile. If you're not preparing for a TEOTWAWKI situation, it may be something that you want to add to your food stockpile when it's on sale. If you're planning for a time when the primary income earner will be seasonally laid off, you need to remember to include that person for lunch, especially if that's something you don't normally do because they are at work.

You also have to decide, especially if you're planning for a large group, just how strict you should be with serving sizes. Nutritional guidelines state that a moderately active 28-year-old woman should have 2,000 calories per day, and a moderately active 28-year-old man should have 2600 calories per day. Your goal should be to make sure as many of those calories as possible come from vegetables, whole grains, and lean proteins, but you must also make the decision as to whether or not you are going to allow extra servings. Is the 28-year-old man extra hungry today because he did more physical labor? Will an extra slice of bread take him over the 2600 calories you planned for him to consume today, and is that going to leave you short of the allotted food for the week or the month? Will you take the time to measure out each serving of food to make sure that each person only gets an exact amount of food? If you're able to, you should try to plan at least 10% more calories, per day, than those guidelines suggest. If you have extras, they can either be consumed as leftovers, fed to farm animals, or used as bait when hunting. Again, there's a fine line between extras and waste, and if you're in a position where you need to stockpile food for any reason, you should plan to avoid waste as often as possible.

If you're stockpiling for a poverty situation, you will probably be able to save leftovers, and should plan to use them for later lunches or as parts of different meals. A beef roast makes great soup or beef stroganoff later in the week. But if you're prepping for a TEOTWAWKI situation, you won't be able to refrigerate those leftovers, and storing them in a root cellar could lead to pest infestation. In that case, you could can the leftovers, over an open fire, or on a woodstove, you could feed a neighbor, or you could use the leftovers for animal feed or bait. When prepping for a TEOTWAWKI situation, you may find it useful to cut meats into smaller portions or can most of it ahead of time to reduce your waste later on.

Chapter Two: How to obtain the food you'll need

Determining what is best to buy, where, is one of the most complex issues when you're prepping for long-term food storage. Supermarket, warehouse clubs, and farmer's markets are great choice for food you can't grow yourself-or grow enough of for long-term preps. Growing your own offers other advantages as well.

Supermarkets offer a few distinct advantages over warehouse stores when it comes to long term food stockpiling: size of the units, store brands, and coupons. When you're looking at canned condensed soup, it's easier to store smaller cans than the larger ones available at the warehouse stores. Something like condensed soup can't be easily repackaged if you can't use the entire container quickly, and it can be difficult to carry a large number ten can through your house if you're weaving around small children and newborn puppies. Store brands often carry a substantial savings per unit, even when compared to warehouse club prices. And coupons are an amazing tool, giving you the ability to stock up on name brand products at rock bottom prices. Shopping at a supermarket also brings with it a definite set of challenges. First off, you may be limited in what quantities you can buy. Many stores limit quantities to make sure they don't run out of a specific item. On the other side of that coin, a store may be out of an item you want to buy.

Despite the bad side of supermarket shopping, the unit sizes are definitely a plus when it comes to many items, especially if you won't be feeding an army. The supermarket gives you the opportunity to buy in the sizes you need rather than the food service sizes that are often what's available at warehouse clubs. If canned soups, fruits, and vegetables are part of your preparations, it's a good idea to buy them at your supermarket. You can even buy single servings of many of these items, which are ideal if there are just a couple of people in your household, although they are more expensive in the long run.

If your budget is tight, supermarket store brands often offer the best deal in the smaller sizes, on a regular basis. In other words, supermarket store brands don't often go on sale, but when you need something to fill out your stockpile, and you can't wait for it to be on sale, buying the store brand is usually the way to go, especially with the basics like canned soups, tomato products, and fruits. There is usually very little difference in the quality of these canned items when compared to the name brands. Supermarket store brands are also the best way to stock up on baking staples like sugar, flour, cornstarch and salt. While the name brands of these items go on sale, they don't do so very often, and without careful watching and coupon gathering, the store brands are still a better deal.

Of course, coupon shopping is often the best way to get the most bang for your buck. Paired with in store sales, manufacturer's coupons can be a great way to bring down prices on your favorite name brand items, and using them can quickly grow your stockpile. However, coupons take time to clip and organize, and coupon shopping can be frustrating if your item is out of stock or difficult to locate. If you have time, though, by matching coupons with store sales you can see prices that are up to 75% off of the regular price. That's a pretty significant savings, and a great way to build your stockpile.

Fresh produce can also be a good purchase at your supermarket, if several factors fall into place:
- You can't grow the produce yourself
- You can't get the produce locally at a Farmer's Market
- The produce is on sale for cheaper than you could get it at the warehouse club, if you have a membership
- You have the means to preserve the produce

Many fruits and vegetables may meet all of these criteria, depending on where you live. If you can afford to buy organic fruits and vegetables, chances are, you're going to find them for a more reasonable price at the supermarket than at the Farmer's Market, although if you are buying in bulk, you may be able to negotiate for a better price at the Farmer's Market. Organic produce doesn't go on sale as often as non-organic, so if you have the time to process fifty pounds of potatoes or tomatoes, try the Farmer's Market instead of the supermarket. If you're buying at the Farmer's Market, chances are the produce was still on the plant or in the ground twelve hours before you bought it. The same cannot be said of most supermarket produce, even when it's organic and local.

Of course, not everyone can afford to buy organic. It's okay if your food choices can't go that route. By stockpiling, you may find that you're able to switch to buying organic over time. When you're not buying organic, you may find that the supermarket is a great resource for adding fresh produce, that you process at home, to your stockpile.

Walking into a warehouse club for the first time can be an overwhelming experience. Some clubs are larger than entire malls, and within their walls are literally almost everything you'll ever need, from birth to death. From diapers to caskets, you can find, or order, almost anything at a warehouse club.

There are a lot of good buys here, especially if you're shopping for a family or large group. However, when shopping at a warehouse club, you need two things: space to store your stockpile, and the time to repackage a good deal of what you buy.

Produce can be a great deal at warehouse clubs, if you have the ability to preserve what you buy, or you will use it before it goes bad. Prices are often very reasonable, but the produce is rarely local. However, you can get out-of-season produce for a much better price than you can at the supermarket, as long as you are prepared to buy in larger quantities.

Warehouse clubs are also the best place to buy important pantry items like rice, beans, most cooking oils, and coffee. This is also where you want to purchase your stocks of pre-packaged items like granola bars, and breakfast cereals. And because warehouse clubs market to restaurants, this is a great place to stock up on single serving packets of items that would require refrigeration after opening, like mayonnaise. Paper goods, including storage bags, are also often a good deal at warehouse clubs.

In most regions, with good soil and inexpensive water, growing your own fruits and vegetables is by far the least expensive way to stockpile food for the long term. Even if you have limited space, you can use alternate growing methods to improve the quality of food you're able to provide for your family and yourself.

Growing your own food doesn't have to mean selling your home and moving out to the country. Even suburban and urban homes can grow at least some of their food. Container gardening, vertical gardening, and putting chickens in your back yard or apartment rooftop can be viable ways to grow at least some of your own food without having much land to call your own.

Chapter Three: The List - The best methods for obtaining the foods you need to build your stockpile

This list will primarily focus on whole, basic foods. Obviously, if you're including prepared food in your preps, you're buying those at the best price you can find, straight off of store shelves. Determining the best methods for stocking up on whole foods can be a bit more difficult. This list is a guide to help you determine which methods are right for you.

When you're doing your shopping, you need to choose simple, utility type foods. You may have a favorite source for your cinnamon or a favorite variety of heirloom tomato. While these are tasty, in a poverty or TEOTWAWKI situation, you want simple and hardy-and your budget may dictate what you can buy. When choosing your foods and/or seeds, choose varieties that will store well, and that don't need special growing environments or extra attention. You may be doing extra work, and while gardening will have an entirely new meaning when it needs to yield enough food for your family for a year, your time there may still be limited.

The produce aisle – Clearly, growing your own is the best way to go here. However, not everyone has the space, or the time to process the food for long-term storage.

Potatoes - These dehydrate well, and store well through the winter, without processing, in the right conditions. Buy instant potato flakes for mashed potatoes or to bulk up bread recipes, and boxed potatoes for different flavors. Dehydrated potatoes go well in soups and stews.

Onions - These dehydrate well and store well through the winter. They can also be diced and then frozen, but are stringy and limp when thawed so make sure your dices are fairly small. Do not buy pre-frozen.

Lettuces - Most lettuces do not store well. Spinach, diced and frozen, makes a good addition to soups and sauces, but won't be good plain.

Celery - Celery both dehydrates and freezes well.

Carrots - Dehydrate, can or freeze. If you can't grow your own, you'll get the most bang for your buck by buying canned.

Green Beans - Freeze or can. If you can't grow your own, buy canned.

Yams or sweet potatoes - DO NOT CAN. Your best bet here is to buy canned.

Corn - Freeze, can, or dehydrate. If you have a wheat grinder, dehydrate plenty of corn for corn meal.

Melons - Pickle or dehydrate for a sweet treat.

Peppers - Dice and Freeze or dehydrate. The flavor and heat intensity will increase with freezing.

Cucumbers - Pickle

Cabbage - Ferment

Berries - Freeze, dehydrate, or can. These can best as jams, jellies or syrups.

Bananas - Dehydrate, or freeze in pre-measured amounts for recipes such as banana bread.

Squash - Many squashes cannot be canned due to their density. Freezing is best for most squash, and pumpkin is much easier to buy in a can at the supermarket.

Peaches - Can or Freeze

Apricots - Can or Freeze

Cherries - Can or freeze

Tomatoes - Can, freeze or dehydrate. Again, with tomatoes, you'll save time and frustration by buying already canned products at the supermarket. Skinning alone takes hours of time for large batches of tomatoes.

Apples - Can, freeze or dehydrate; can also be fermented for cider, although this takes up a lot of space.

Pears - Can, freeze or dehydrate.

Citrus - Can juice in ½ pint containers, and dehydrate zest.

Broccoli - Freeze or dehydrate.

Cauliflower - Freeze.

Beans (other than green beans) - Don't produce much when grown for the space they require, buy dry and prepare from that state, or can. Do not can refried beans.

Peas - Shell, then dehydrate or can.

Grapes - Freeze, dehydrate, or can as juice, jam or jelly. Can also be used for wine, which would be great for barter in a TEOTWAWKI situation.

Garlic - Dehydrate. Do not can or infuse in oil, as garlic is very susceptible to botulism.

The Baking Aisle – Most of the products we bake with are not far removed from their whole sources. Using whole-wheat flour takes practice and finesse. Begin experimenting with whole grains as you're building your stockpile, as whole-wheat flour tastes different, and bakes different, than store bought enriched white flour. An essential purchase for a TEOTWAWKI situation is a hand crank grain mill. This will allow you to grow or store whole grains and grind them into flour when you need them. Flours go rancid quicker than their whole grain counterparts, so it's better to store the whole grains than flour, especially if you're planning for a scenario where there is no power, or limited power, to keep things cool. Keeping things dry is also very important. You don't want those whole grains getting moldy. It can often be difficult to spot on whole grains, and ergot poisoning can have long-term catastrophic effects. Ergotism is believed to be the cause of the mass hysteria and physical symptoms that led to the Salem witch trials.

Sugar - Buy 25-pound bags, and re-package into gallon or quart zip type bags, double bagging for security. Pack those into a 5-gallon bucket with Diatomaceous Earth.

Flours - Buy 25-pound bags, and re-package into gallon or quart zip type bags, double bagging for security. Pack those into a 5-gallon bucket with Diatomaceous Earth. It's better, however, to buy and store whole grains, grinding either as you need them or for a week at a time.

Whole Grains - Buy 25 or 50 pound bags, and re-package into gallon or quart zip type bags, double bagging for security. Pack those into a 5-gallon bucket with Diatomaceous Earth.

Oils, lard, shortening - Buy shelf stable oils and solid fats that are long lasting and better for you. Stick with corn, olive, lard and coconut. Oils will go rancid, so store them in an environment that is as cool as possible, such as a root cellar or basement. Once the containers are opened, move them into a dryer area, and keep them as cool as possible.

Spices - Buy only what you can use in a year, as most herbs and spices will lose their flavor in that time, although they can safely sit on a shelf for five years. Even if on a small scale, plan for an herb garden and to grow basics like onions and garlic. It's amazing what some flavor will do for an appetite in a TEOTWAWKI situation.

Salt - Buy plenty, and keep it dry.

Baking powder - Buy plenty, and keep it dry. You'll be using this for bread rising once your yeast dies.

Yeast - Freeze for longer life.

Baking soda - Buy plenty, then buy some more. Baking soda has a myriad of uses besides baking, and you'll want plenty on hand. To keep dry, store in original packaging, then zip type bags, in 5 gallon buckets with diatomaceous earth.

Cornstarch - Like baking soda, buy plenty, then buy some more. Cornstarch is an excellent skin remedy for chafing and heat rash, and since you'll be doing more manual labor, it's excellent to keep on hand for those ailments.

Baking mixes - Baking mixes have some of the highest mark ups in the grocery business. Learning how to make your own saves you money, but is often time consuming. Also, the raw ingredients may not last as long as the baking mix when they are sitting on your shelf because your raw ingredients have no preservatives. While products with no preservatives are better for you in the long run, it shortens the amount of time you can safely store these products. If you're storing for a situation where your income would be reduced, find recipes online for your favorite baking mixes and use the money you'll save on other items. If you're stockpiling for a TEOTWAWKI situation, you'll want to make baking mixes a part of your preps.

Chocolate Chips and other silly baking additions - These are very necessary stock ups. Food fatigue is a very real issue in survival type situations, and our bodies may actually give us negative reactions such as nausea to a food we've been eating a lot of, which can be deadly in a survival type situation. Being able to add chocolate chips to pancakes or butterscotch chips to farina cereal can change the flavor of the food so that the body is less likely to reject it. So while these may be silly or non-essential items, you should have some on hand. They are also great for barter. Store them in the freezer while you can, and then the coolest environment you can find, double bagged, in 5 gallon buckets with diatomaceous earth.

The Dairy Aisle - Buying a cow is a great idea-in theory. In reality, a single cow takes at least eleven acres of quality grass to feed. If you don't have eleven acres, you're buying expensive hay, in addition to water, medications, and vet care for the cow. While it is a worthy investment if you have the space, make sure you do research on different breeds to determine which types are beneficial to your needs, and that you will have access to a bull during breeding season.

Milk - Buy powdered, and vanilla extract. It will never taste the same, but it will at least be drinkable with the addition of the vanilla. Powdered milk also works fine for baking and cooking, except for making pudding and gravy. Milk does freeze very well if you pour a cup or so out of the container prior to freezing, but it's impossible to store in large quantities.

Butter - Freeze, then keep as cool as possible. You may see information online regarding canning butter or ghee, but this cannot be safely done at home. You can buy commercially canned butter.

Margarine - Skip it if you can. Sticks freeze well, but you're better off buying butter, which will give better results when thawed. At half the price of butter it is a tempting addition to your stockpile, but it has no nutritional or long-term storage merit.

Eggs - Scramble, mix with a pinch of salt per egg, and freeze. Use ice cube trays for single eggs, small plastic containers for batches of three eggs for baking, and plastic zip type bags for large batches for cooking breakfast. Once the smaller measures are frozen solid, remove from containers and bag. While you may see information online regarding dehydrating eggs, it's not something that can be safely done at home. You can buy freeze-dried eggs online, which are much better for longer shelf life, but are rather expensive. Buying chickens is a viable option for many; an increasing number of municipalities are legalizing back yard chickens, making it possible for almost anyone to have fresh eggs. However, if you're planning on having chickens for the long term, you will need a rooster, and plenty of room for them to graze, unless you're also going to stockpile chicken feed. You'll also need space to allow them to brood, as established flocks will often peck chicks to death. Consider building chicken tractors to keep them somewhat free ranging but still protecting them from predators.

Sour cream - Does not store well, long term, in any form. You can buy powdered sour cream.

Buttermilk - The fats separate when frozen. You can buy frozen buttermilk, which works well for baking.

Cream cheese - It can be frozen, but loses the consistency for using raw. Works well in recipes that call for it to be fully cooked.

Cottage cheese - Does not store well, long term, in any form.

Hard cheeses - Hard cheeses freeze well, although frozen cheese is best cooked or melted rather than served raw. Grate, then freeze, as the cheese gets crumbly when frozen so it will not handle well if frozen in a block or in slices. American cheese does not freeze well. Velveeta, cheese whiz, and other types of processed cheeses are shelf stable for years.

Meats - Raising your own meat is a great goal, but something that requires good breeding stock, and a lot of land. In the long run, it may be cheaper to can or otherwise preserve your meat rather than trying to grow it, especially if you're living on a small homestead.

Chicken - Roast, strip the meat, then boil the carcass to make a broth. Can with the meat for bases for soups and stews; can without the meat for chicken broth to add to other recipes. You can buy canned chicken for use in recipes such as casseroles where you don't necessarily need the broth.

Beef Steak - Stick to cheaper cuts of steak like sirloin or round, and use for jerky. These steaks freeze well and often go on sale for reasonable prices.

Beef Stew Meat - With oxtail or other bones, make broth without any thickeners, and can for base for soups and stews. Only buy on sale, as meat sold as stew meat is often highly marked up.

Ground Beef - Cook as usual, with no seasoning, drain off all fat and rinse, then can. Buy the leanest ground beef you can find for long-term storage, because you need to have as little fat as possible in the product that you can. The more fat that is in a product, the quicker it will go rancid, even when properly canned. It is important that any meats you process in this manner are skimmed of as much fat as possible.

Beef Brisket or Roast - Cook in crockpot, can with resulting broth for base for meat and gravy meals, stroganoff, or soups. Brisket is normally priced at half the price of roast, and often goes on sale around Memorial Day. While not as tender as roast, it is a suitable substitute for many meals when slow cooked. This is not corned beef brisket, which can also be slow cooked and canned.

Pork Roast - Cook in crockpot, can with resulting broth for base for meat and gravy meals, or soups. Pork roast often goes on sale in early May and makes a rich, flavorful broth.

Pork Ribs - Cook in crockpot, can with resulting broth for base for meat and gravy meals, or soups like green chili. Ribs are higher in fat than many pork cuts and while they are often inexpensive cuts, they should not be your first choice for canning unless absolutely necessary.

Ham - Buy canned. Whole hams freeze well but modern smoking methods do not allow for preservation outside of freezing. Smoking is one of the least reliable ways of meat preservation.

Bacon - Freeze. Due to the high fat content, bacon is not suitable for canning.

Fish - Buy canned tuna, albacore and salmon. Salmon cans well but many other fish varieties end up very mushy when home canned. Freezes well.

Lamb - Freeze, or can.

Venison - Freeze, or can like beef. If you live rurally or even in the suburbs, hunting will be a great way to increase your protein consumption in a TEOTWAWKI scenario. It's a good idea to build a hoist mechanism that will hold enough weight for you to skin out an elk, if they are anywhere near your area. While you can have several days of fresh meat from a kill, you can, can the remainder over an open fire if need be, for long-term food preservation even while in the TEOTWAWKI scenario. This way none of your catch is going to waste.

Pork-based sausages - Freeze. Due to their high fat content, pork-based sausages are not suitable for canning. For long-term storage, grind your meat as for sausage, but without adding the fat. Can as you would ground beef. When serving, season with appropriate spices and serve as sausage gravy, crumbles in a casserole, or as Italian sausage in pasta sauce.

Staples

Rice - Buy in 25 or 50-pound bags, double bag in zip type bags, and store in 5 gallon buckets with diatomaceous earth. Also consider buying flavored rices to break up the monotony of your diet.

Coffee - Absolutely essential, both as a prep and as a barter item. Calculate how much you drink in a year, then purchase triple that. You'll have two years' worth of coffee and another year's worth to barter with.

Peanut Butter - Buy plenty, in 16 ounce jars.

Jelly - Buy or make plenty, in 16 ounce jars.

Honey - You cannot stockpile too much honey. It's a versatile sweetener, and works well to dress wounds.

Miscellaneous

Juices - These take up a lot of space in your stores, but can be a valuable source of needed liquids. If you have the room, stock enough for a gallon per week per four people.

Alcohol - In stressful situations, some people drink to help relieve stress. Alcohol can also be used to calm down someone who is upset, as a sedative, or to clean out a wound. You certainly don't want someone who is used to having a few drinks after work coming off alcohol cold turkey, either. Alcohol's most useful property, however, is as a barter tool. People will perceive it as a need. If you have it, you can use it to obtain something you need.

Soda - Absolutely skip stockpiling soda. It has no nutritional value. If someone in your family has a caffeine addiction, stockpile tea bags and work on switching them from soda to tea. Not only does it have less caffeine, making it a good way to taper down, it takes up far less room to stockpile.

Water - You will not stockpile enough water. If you live near a water source, buy a good filter and some good 50-gallon storage barrels. If you don't live near a water source, buy a good filter, more 50-gallon storage barrels to store rain and snow, and enough water in one-gallon containers for three months. The minimum standards for water storage are one gallon, per person, per day. If you have small children, or someone elderly, store three gallons for each of them, per day. You'll also need water for pets and livestock. Refill two and three liter soda bottles, but don't refill milk containers because it's nearly impossible to get all of the milk residue off the plastic, and that can contaminate your water supply. Save the milk containers for portable hot houses for your garden.

Paper goods - Don't neglect purchasing necessary paper goods for cooking. You'll need aluminum foil, plastic wrap, muffin tin liners, paper plates, bowls, cups, and plastic silverware. The less dishes you have to wash, the less water you will use.

Vitamins - Since you will be eating a calorie restricted diet, you will need to have a good stock of vitamins on hand to make sure you're getting your necessary nutrients.

Condiments - These are extras, but will help fight off food fatigue. Having mayo and pickles on the shelves is going to make those Vienna sausages much more palatable, because now they can be made into a sandwich instead of eaten straight out of the can.

Infant Formula - While "breast is best" takes on a whole new meaning in a TEOTWAWKI situation, as well as in a poverty type situation, sometimes things happen that require a change in plans. If someone who is of childbearing age is going to be with you for the long haul, it is a good idea to stock up on infant formula. If you end up not using the formula, it could become a valuable barter item. If you stockpile infant formula, make sure to donate it to a homeless shelter or food pantry at least two months before its expiration date, and get a receipt for the donation. The tax write off for the charitable contribution will help fund your restocking of this expensive prep item.

On buying processed foods - You're going to buy processed foods. Your preps are your business and no one is going to judge you because you have a case of canned ravioli or blue box macaroni and cheese in your pantry. If these are items you feel your family needs, then stockpile them. While ideally your preps are as natural and nutritious as possible, stockpiling familiar foods helps ward off food fatigue and makes it easier to take care of your family. It may also be essential to have quick meals available in the event that the head chef is busy tending livestock, in the garden, or dealing with an emergency. Just try to make sure that the bulk of your food preps, over time, are foods that are not heavily processed. There is a comfort in these foods for many people, but often the nutrition leaves much to be desired, and that's not something you want to skimp on, in a TEOTWAWKI scenario.

While food preservation is a great skill to learn, it takes practice to get it right, and time to build up a stock of home canned "convenience" food, or any type of food, to be truthful. Sometimes, canned processed food is a way to fill that gap to give your family a more balanced selection of food choices. Frankly, if TEOTWAWKI happened tomorrow, you would rather have a case of ravioli on hand than nothing. You should not feel bad because you have store brand canned tomato soup that you bought on sale rather than home canned tomato soup in pretty mason jars. You should feel a sense of accomplishment that you have provided a good meal starter for your family, no matter what the source. But as your stockpile grows, try to add foods with a higher nutritional value.

Conclusion

No matter what type of event you are prepping for, it's important to go about it in an organized way. Otherwise, you'll end up with a lot of bits and pieces of many meals, with nothing to really put together into something nutritious and edible-both very important facets of any meal, especially in either a poverty or TEOTWAWKI situation.

While there is something to be said for "hunger adds flavor," putting together a nutritious, yet edible meal insures that the people you're prepping for are both sated and fueled for what could be very hard manual labor. It's important that you find a good balance as you stockpile food.

Methods of food preservation are as unique as those that practice them. Not all of them will work for you and your family. It's perfectly all right if most of your stockpile is built from items you bought, on sale and with a coupon, at the supermarket, just as it's also perfectly okay if you love getting up before the sun to go milk your cow every day. You have to find what works best for your situation.

Canning is a valuable food preservation skill, and its importance not only for starting but for maintaining your food stockpile cannot be overlooked. If you learn how to can over an open fire or a wood stove, you can further preserve hunting bounty or shared food so that you will be able to get even more meals over time. Hunting isn't predictable, and in a TEOTWAWKI situation, close local game will exhaust itself in a suburban area. In a poverty situation, hunting is a great way to help fill the freezer as winter sets in, but the lack of predictability means that you could invest in a gun and a hunting license only to come home with no meat. But if you have the ability to can any hunting catch that is made, your food security lengthens over time and will continue to grow even if the likelihood of grocery stores reopening for business is minimal. Canning is such a valuable skill, in fact, that any preparation for TEOTWAWKI is not complete without its' mastery, because with no power, there will be no other way to insure a protein source over long cold winters without becoming migratory, like the animals you will be hunting.

Finally, even with the help of this guide, prepping or stockpiling food may seem a bit overwhelming to you especially at first. It's important to remember that everyone once started somewhere. Remember the tips that were mentioned in this guide.
- Set reasonable goals. It's great that you want to have one year's worth of food on hand. But it's better to plan for three days, then seven, then fourteen, and continue growing both your stockpile and your goal, than to try to coordinate the logistics of buying a year's worth of anything all at once.

- Start small. It's okay if, after your first week of shopping, you've only purchased enough supplies for one meal. You're working with what you can obtain. If it's October as you read this and you didn't have a garden this year, you're certainly going to have to have a major part of your stockpile come from the grocery store, for the first few months of your stockpiling adventure. Even with coupons and store sales, that can add up.

- Learn a new skill. If you can learn to can or dehydrate, you've just exponentially increased the amount of food you are able to stockpile for your family.

- Make your budget work for you. If you normally budget $30 a month for eating out, make home-made pizza or grab something from the dollar menu, and use the remainder of the money for prep items.

- If you get an income tax refund, use it to buy prep items like a good dehydrator, canning equipment, storage bags and buckets, etc. If you don't get an income tax refund, set aside $10 or $20 per week to buy these items.

- Make a plan, and stick to it. Your plan should reflect your goals, how you will obtain your food, your available skill set, your available tools, how you will preserve your food, and your budget.

Preparing for the future, no matter what your reason or what you're preparing for, does take hard work and diligence, but it doesn't have to be overwhelming or confusing! In time, the baby steps that you're taking now will turn into larger steps and you will begin to see real achievement. It brings a sense of accomplishment when you walk into your food storage area and realize that you have a month, or three months', worth of food on hand. As your preps continue to grow, you will find it easier to use what you have and fill in the gaps as things go on sale. Where before you could only buy one or two of a particular item that was on sale, at some point you'll be able to buy ten or twelve, because you will be paying full price less often.

While canning is the game changer in terms of long-term preps, growing your own food also greatly increases your chances for long-term food security. Whether you are prepping to avoid poverty cycles, or for an end of the world scenario, the skills, ability, space, and tools to grow your own food will substantially benefit your efforts. While it may be impossible to grow all of your own food in the city, there are many examples of people who have used the space they have in a creative manner, allowing them to grow more food than most people think is possible on city lots.

With the right mindset, prepping can be something that becomes a habit, rather than a hobby. If you are always in "prep mode," you will always be looking for ways to build your food stockpile in the most inexpensive ways possible. Once you've developed this mindset, it is much easier to plan for extremely long-term preps.

Again, this is a mindset that will take months, if not years, to develop.

You should build your stockpile at your own pace, using your goals and your budget as a guide. Make the attempt to work towards zero waste and purchasing the healthiest foods that you can afford, for your family. Baby steps will guide your way in the beginning, but in time, you will find yourself making great strides to lead the lifestyle of your goals!

The Nomad Prepper: A Guide to Mobile Survival

Introduction

Survival is a tricky thing – everybody has a different take on how to do it, but in reality, it can be a whole lot simpler than most "Doomsday Prepper" folks seem to think it is. We may be thrust into a survival situation by any of a number of different situations: economic collapse, both globally and locally, a natural disaster of epic proportions, terrorism and increased warfare, and on and on. We can't know exactly when or how a survival situation will occur, but history tells us that it's only a matter of time before we, and our loved ones, will be in need of survival skills.

A survival situation occurs when you cannot rely upon human civilization, either because it is nowhere to be found or because it simply can't help you. Either way, the safety net of civilization is unavailable to you. In this type of situation, it is best to keep your wits about you, use what you can and know how to defend yourself. If you are trying to survive, strangers can be your worst enemy or your best friend, so be wary, but don't be stupid. The first thing to keep in mind in a survival situation is that the world is not black and white – if you come across other people, be aware that they are also just trying to survive.

You don't need to be predatory to stay alive; you just need to be resourceful. Work with what is available to you and keep a clear head – panic is your worst enemy and will get you killed. If you are surviving just with what you have and you are out in the wild, know that anything can happen; you need to be prepared for any and everything, and that is what this whole guide is about.

You often hear all of these grand ideas about prepping: how you should be stocking up on non-perishable food items, building a secure panic room or a fallout shelter in your home or on your property, and planning to stay in one spot so that you and your family will be safe and sound while whatever danger there is can pass right by. This might work for a while, in certain situations, but some may not call it survival, so much as hiding. It will work in some situations, for some people, but there is another way of survival that is often overlooked: Mobile Survival.

The fact is, human beings are nomads; it is how we have evolved, why we are built the way we are and perhaps it is even the reason we go a little stir-crazy if we stay in the same place too long. Movement is now, and always has been, the human survival strategy that works the best – not to say it isn't dangerous, but so is staying put. However, the biggest downside to becoming nomadic after a societal collapse is this: constant movement is tiring. It will wear on you. But take heed: there are ways you can combat this downside, to ensure that the mobile lifestyle continues to work for you and your family. For example, there is nothing that says you can't stop for some respite for a little while, especially in regions with bad storms or freezing winters, in which case finding some long-term shelter and stocking up on food is a very good idea for waiting out the rougher seasons. There are many tips and tricks like these below, which will help you decide if the nomad life and Mobile Survival are the right plans for you and your family.

So if you are into the nomad lifestyle, you will need to be prepared for what that means in terms of relinquishing any material possessions you cannot carry on your back, testing yourself mentally and physically outside of civilization, and facing dangerous (even potentially life-threatening) obstacles. As an avid Prepper, someone who is prepared for all situations, and a DIY enthusiast, I will be sharing some helpful tips on how to be a Nomad Prepper, and for keeping you and your family safe on the road, no matter the situation.

Keys to Being a Nomad Prepper

As with regular prepping, there are certain ideas and keys that are fundamental when one starts to think about mobile prepping. These are the very base techniques and ideas that will help you establish a foundation of knowledge and skills that will come in handy if and when the need arises. Below we'll take a look at these areas, and explore them a bit more in-depth.

Know your environment:

The most important thing for both stationary and mobile prepping is this: Know your environment. Your prepping plans will change dramatically depending on which part of the country you are in, whether you are rural or urban, and which season of the year it is. You cannot plan to survive for very long anywhere, if you don't know what is around you and how to interact with what you see. The biggest part of your preparation should be familiarizing yourself with the local wildlife, plants, animals, edible or medicinal herbs, and any dangers or advantages specific to your local area. Know what grows when, mating seasons of animals, harvest seasons, animal habitats, indigenous species, what you can use, and how you can use it. Watch the animals; see where they go, what they eat, where they drink. Know the seasons and weather patterns. Learn to look for changes in the sky, moon cycles and cloud formations – observe how these effect the environment around you. Take the time to study now, as this will pay off greatly in the future.

Another important aspect of knowing your environment is knowing the other people who share that space. Get to know the people around (if any) and what they are like. Naturally, people are going to vary widely and great distinctions can be made between urban and rural environments. In any case, it is always beneficial to make friends where you can in a survival situation. You don't have to like a person to benefit from the skills and experience they can bring to a survival situation. Television has taught us that human beings are essentially selfish and opportunistic, that survival is a competitive sport wherein the best man wins; this is false.

Certainly there are opportunistic people out there who will take advantage of the situation and go out of their way to hurt others in order to help themselves. In a real survival situation, this behavior should be what gets those guys killed; however, they still exist and it is your job as a survivor to understand that survival is not just a reality TV thought experiment but something very real, which requires cooperation instead of competition. Human beings are social creatures, we have always relied upon one another and this should be no different in a survival scenario. Learn to pick up on antisocial behaviors and don't allow yourself to be taken advantage of. You don't need or want "that guy" with you and you don't need to be "that guy" to stay alive. Leverage the skills, knowledge, and resources of the good people around you, and you'll have a much greater chance of survival.

Have Hideouts and Squats:

Squats can be thought of as your home-away-from-home. Just because you are a nomad doesn't mean you don't need a home base. You can benefit greatly from a temporary shelter, where you can eat in peace, store your pack while you're out scavenging, or just to grab a quick rest. No matter where you are, this is entirely necessary. The easiest way to secure a home base is to form a squat (and don't give me that "legality" crap, you are trying to survive). An abandoned house is perfect – you don't have to build it and after you have been on the trail for so long, you know you will want a nice roof over your head. Of course, you don't have to form a squat on your own; you might find one already in existence, if you know what to look for.

Not too long ago, there used to be a simple system of symbols that travelers and transients used to communicate with one another, both out in the wild and in the midst of civilization. What came to be known as "the hobo code" was created in the 1930's by vagabond workers who would hop trains back and forth between cities looking for work. While many of these signs have either changed a lot since their inception or have stopped being used altogether, there is one symbol that lives on today – the squat symbol (see right).

If you see that symbol etched into a door or spray-painted on the side of a building, you have found the right place. If there are people there, don't be a jerk, respect their space and maybe they will let you stay a few nights. The squat symbol is an easy and efficient way to communicate with other travelers and point them toward safe shelter. If you do form your own squat, make sure to open it to others, keeping general safety in mind, of course (in a truly desperate situation, there may be others who would open it to themselves anyway).

You can (and should) have multiple bases around the region you are traveling in for easy access. All of these should preferably be accessible to other weary travelers needing a place to stop and rest awhile. (Note: This isn't just a cop out place to run off and hole up, but it can be useful during cold winters or unbearable heat). This place can have a consistent stock of non-perishable food items or just a storage room that can be filled by travelers at their convenience when preparation for a retreat from the elements is necessary. Brutal cold or brutal heat will diminish the amount of food available and can also be dangerous to any who are too heavily exposed; keep that in mind at all times.

The purpose of having squats is securing access to consistent and stable places to go in emergency situations. Besides abandoned houses, you can look for closed businesses, warehouses, garages, sheds, etc. On top of offering a roof over your head for a night or two, these are places to grow food and medicinal herbs. Horticulture is the food production strategy of nomads, as it is based upon plant growth in nature (what grows most commonly near what and how they appear to benefit each other). This is where sister planting comes from (the practice of planting certain foods together to create higher yields and healthier plants). I strongly suggest researching horticulture, as this is an incredibly efficient way to grow a lot of food in very little space. It is simple enough to find many in-depth sources at your local library, and the time spent there will be well worth it. Planting seeds along your trails may also be useful, as you can always come back to different locations at different points to get exactly what you need.

Prepare for Mobile Prepping:

Before you set out, you will need something to carry your stuff in. I've met all kinds of travelers, many of who needlessly overburden themselves with gigantic hiking packs larger than they are. Sure, one of those will carry all you need and more, and if you happen to be built like a linebacker, then this type of pack might just be the one for you. However, for those individuals who aren't especially large or muscular, a smaller pack will do just as well, and probably even better.

In general, the less weight you have to carry, the better, and if you are going to be carrying everything you have on your back everywhere you go, you want a pack that is suitable for your individual size and strength in order to avoid needless injury. Any sporting goods store with hiking supplies should carry a number of good packs in all sizes, and you can certainly find a huge selection online these days as well. Pick the one you think is best for you, make sure it has enough room for everything you will be carrying and check to see if there are extra pockets and compartments for smaller things that you will be needing to keep handy. Remember, the more compact, the better – a good hiking pack can run anywhere from $200-$500, but it is worth it. This will be your main equipment for survival - Don't skimp out on quality. Some hiking packs don't have a place to secure a sleeping bag or bedroll, so you will probably want to find one that does. Above all, check to make sure you adjust your pack to distribute weight evenly. Without proper weight distribution, you can seriously hurt yourself on the trail – this is very important. Try it on, load it up with some good weight, and carry it around for an hour or two. You need to make sure that it holds up to the weight and that it is still comfortable after an extended period of use. Don't just buy one for the looks – functionality is the most important factor for choosing the right bag.

Now that you have a bag, you need stuff to put in it. Of course you will need clothes, but this is a survival situation and we're not going for fancy, but utilitarian – here's a basic checklist for the clothing you will need:

- Two outfits: the one you are wearing and one in your pack. One of these should be light – for spring and summer weather, and the other warm – for fall and winter weather (no worries, you will have opportunities to make new clothes or patch the old ones up). This is region dependent, so if you're going mobile in the south of Georgia, you can get away with one light and one semi-light outfit; if you're surviving in Montana, you're going to need some more heavy-duty winter clothes.

- Shoes: there is no reason to wear any shoes that aren't hiking boots, preferably waterproof and insulated (steel-toe might be good also, but not necessary). A good pair of hiking boots can run anywhere from $50-$200. Imagine how long you will be on your feet every day though, and you will quickly see that this is one area you do not want to skimp on. Buy high-quality and built to last, and your feet will thank you.

- Long socks, at least three pair (though you can never have enough). These keep your feet safe from all of the walking you'll be doing, from bugs and critters, and provide necessary warmth at night and in colder climates.

-Extra shoe strings: Your hiking boots aren't going to do you any good if you can't even secure them properly. It's the little things like shoe strings that can quickly derail your survival strategy, so pack a few extra. They also have many other uses, so it won't be a waste of space to have a couple packs of them.

- Head covering: a hat or bandana are important, both in hot and cold locales. A hat with a brim will keep the sun out of your eyes and off of your head in the hotter months; a bandana or hat will keep your warmth in during the cold months. This is an often-overlooked clothing item that can make a big difference, so make sure and bring one.

Even for the most hardcore-travelers, hygiene is important – keeping yourself clean will help to keep you healthy. You won't have the same opportunities to shower and brush your teeth and all that good stuff out in the wilderness, but you will want to bathe where you can, so make sure to bring some basic stuff with you for that, including:

- Washrag and/or small towel

- Bar soap (a few). You will run out of this stuff, but it'll last longer than liquid soap and after that, you might find some good plant oils to use (lavender oil is antibacterial, for example).

- A toothbrush or floss. Floss is actually more important than a toothbrush because it is more effective in preventing tooth decay so if you don't floss, start: it breaks up the bacteria cultures between your teeth that feed on sugar and foodstuff and rot your teeth out. (Note: your survival diet will automatically make you cut down on your sugar intake, so your teeth will actually be healthier anyway).

- Toothpaste (optional): you could bring some toothpaste, but you will run out; however, you can make your own toothpaste using crushed up mint leaves and some salt water (more salt, less water).

- Toilet Paper (optional): If you want, take some, but you will run out and have to wipe your ass with leaves or wash off in a nearby body of water. If you are not down with all that, maybe bring an extra washcloth just for this purpose (mark it with sharpie or something); that sounds weird, but just wipe it down on a tough rock after each use and boil it in some water for a few minutes.

You will also want to bring a First Aid kit with you, or compile one yourself. You can buy mini-kits at most camping or outdoor stores, and they should do great for your purposes. If you want to compile one for yourself, that is also quite simple too. This should have gauze, bandages, Band-Aids, Neosporin, etc. You will run out of this stuff, but once you get going, you should be able to make more with whatever materials you collect in your travels.

In a survival situation, everybody cooks. If you don't cook, you will starve, and nobody wants that. Sure, you can eat raw foods and survive for quite some time, forever, if really necessary. But you will miss out on a lot of nutrients and have a much smaller pool of potential foods if you limit yourself to eating raw food only. For cooking on the road, you will need some basic stuff – you don't need all the fancy camping cookware you see at the stores, just the basics (though the more people you have with you, the more you can carry). Here's what you will need for a small set-up:

- Cooking pot, ladle/wooden cooking spoon, mesh wire, eating utensils. Lots of sporting equipment stores and camping supply aisles have camping cookware available for decent prices. Look for a single collapsible pot or deep pan – these can also be found online. Material matters; try to avoid harmful materials like aluminum or Teflon.

- Some dishes (a plate or bowl for each person in your party)

- For forks, spoons and an extra knife, you can find utility knife utensils in the camping aisle of most stores. The novelty of a combination fork/knife/spoon is second only to its practicality.

- Mesh wire, or any type of fabric (i.e., a square cut from an old shirt or pair of pantyhose) that can be secured around the top of your pot for straining. Use this to collect water, and only water, from rivers, lakes, or streams to be boiled and used. (Note: this can also be used as a small fishing net or to protect your face from stinging insects)

- Mortar and pestle: You won't have electricity, so your food processor will be useless. Use a mortar and pestle for crushing up or making a paste out of nuts, berries, herbs, etc. This will make some pretty tough ingredients a lot more useable and widen the net of potential things that you can eat.

- And of course, food: Rice, dried beans, maybe some canned veggies, trail mix, jerky, etc. The key here is to bring things that are small, but filling. You won't be lugging around too much food on a daily basis. Sure, you can keep some larger cans and such at your squat or other hideout locations, but for the daily life, you'll want plenty of trail mix, jerky, protein bars, or any other item that is small, easy to carry, and packed full of vital nutrients to give you energy on your daily journey.

You will also need some foraging and fishing supplies because you will be doing a lot of that, particularly after you have run out of what little food reserves you have brought with you.

- Before you even think about harvesting wild plants of any kind, make sure you either know everything about the plant life in your region or else get yourself some field guides. If you don't know what you are looking for, foraging can become a dangerous way to get food. Eat the wrong plant or explore the wrong area and you can find yourself eating something that makes you very sick, or worse. There are a lot of great resources out there for learning more about which plants are safe to eat, where they are located, and when is the best time of year to find them. Start your research on your specific locale now, and you will make things much easier for yourself later.

- Fishing pole or net. (Note: a fishing net can be made with the mesh fabric I've suggested for straining water. It's important to find items with multiple uses, such as the mesh. The more you can do with the less you have to carry is always the goal.)

- Salt, as much as you can carry: Salt is good for preserving and curing foods and it is an antiseptic and astringent – make yourself some salt water (salty as your tears or as the sea, however you prefer) and you have a great mouthwash or something to clean out open wounds (the latter hurts, but it will slow the bleeding and clean the wound). Salt is another multi-use item and is relatively easy to carry, so plan to pack a fair amount of it.

- Clean water: You and everyone in your party should have at least one water bottle each, preferably a large one, and maybe a jug or something similar on top of that for the group to split. I've met several travelers who carry entire gallons of water on them, but you don't need to do that. It is heavier than you think and will wear you out quickly and slow you down. Two quart-sized bottles are small enough to carry in a pack, won't weigh you down as much and can contain a decent amount to have on reserve (especially if you have about a quart per person). Eventually, you will run out of the clean water you packed, but keep the bottles – you can refill them with water you have collected, just make sure you boil it first so it is clean.

If you choose to bring some camping supplies, such as a tent, you may. These are optional because they are a bit cumbersome and you will be able to make your own in due time, but if this option is available and preferable to you, then get a small tent for 2-4 people that can fit either in or securely on the outside of your pack. The smaller and simpler it is, the easier it will be to carry and set up. (Note: you want to be able to get the smallest tent that you can pack multiple people in). Other than that, you might want some form of bed.

Some people like sleeping bags, but in my experience, I've found sleeping bags to be a giant pain – the material they are most often made out of, while well-insulated, is slippery and annoying. No matter how tightly rolled up your sleeping bag is, it will want to unroll itself as you move, throwing off the weight of your pack and generally inconveniencing you. Beyond that, they only accommodate one person at a time for the most part, which might be fine if you were camping for fun, but this is survival and there is no such thing as privacy anymore. The alternative to a sleeping bag is simple: you can make a good bedroll from at least two insulated blankets (not quilts, they don't need to be thick, just insulated). Fold and roll them up just like a sleeping bag and if you do it right, they will make a smaller, easier to handle package. You can use those extra shoelaces or some good rope to tie up your blankets and you can secure them to the top or bottom of your pack. A bedroll made with blankets can easily accommodate 2-4 people if the blankets are big enough and your traveling party is close-knit enough (and if you aren't at the beginning, you will be eventually). This is important for when it gets cold, which is another reason why I only suggest a small tent or maybe two, depending on the size of your party.

Perhaps the most important thing you can have with you in this type of survival situation is a collection of tools. The more things one tool can be used for, the better. If you are resourceful and know how to use what you have, your tools should be able to get you out of any tight spot, so don't overlook these. Here are some important tools to consider:

- Knives: A good knife should be at the top of your list. These are light, easy to conceal and infinitely useful. At least three would be good, but you'll want at least one at a bare minimum. Specifically, you will want a hunting knife, utility knife, and a skinning knife. That said, don't go crazy; the more knives you have, the more difficult they will be to conceal and while looking cool is nice, utility is more important. You'll want one you can use for hunting, for cutting branches and timber for fires, for cutting clothes and fabrics, and any number of other uses. The bigger and fancier your knives are, the more likely you are to be targeted for weapon theft by opportunistic strangers.

- Whetstone: If you are carrying knives, better keep 'em sharp. No use having a great knife if its blade is so dull that you can't even use it properly.

- Compass: This, in combination with your own variant of the hobo code to mark where you are going and where you have been can ensure that you are never lost. Don't underestimate the importance of keeping tabs on which direction you are heading, and where you've already been. You'll save yourself a lot of time and headaches by knowing your directions.

- Fire-starter: You can start out with a lighter or matches if you want, but both are finite – you will run out sooner or later. You can find flint and magnesium fire-starters in some hardware and outdoor supply stores for less than $5. I'd suggest getting one of those. These last much longer than regular lighters or matches, and are infinitely better at starting fires when and where you need to.

- Hatchet and/or machete: Both have advantages, and if you want to be a badass then you can have both, but it is best just to pick one (one less thing to rust or have to carry). Machetes are made for bushwhacking if you want to make a trail, but a hatchet can be used to collect firewood. Either or both can hang from a hip and neither is particularly heavy, making them both convenient and accessible.

- Rope: This is easily one of the most useful things you can carry. You might want a variety, different thicknesses for different things, but even one good long length of hempen rope, about medium thickness, would be good (doesn't have to be hemp, but it is incredibly durable and will last forever). This will be helpful in constructing all types of shelters, carrying game that you've hunted, repairing things here and there, helping you navigate treacherous heights or lows, and many other things.

- Leather strips: For when you need something more flexible, but just as durable as rope.

Setting Up Camp:

You are packed and prepped, you have gone out into no-man's land and done a little exploring, but now the day is coming to an end and it is time to set up camp. The first thing you need to do is find some shelter (unless you have portable shelter, in which case you just need to find a place to put it). If you have a tent, you will want to find a good clear area. Find the flattest patch of ground you can and throw your tent down. Keep in mind when you are placing your tent, most tents are made of tarp or a similar material and are incredibly flammable so make sure it is not going to be too near your fire.

If you don't have a tent, there are a couple of options – you can build a lean-to, which requires gathering materials (driftwood is a good option if it is available); or in the right terrain, you can find shelter in a nearby cave. Building a lean-to is fairly straightforward: assess your situation and your surroundings, try to find a large, healthy tree to use as your base and go gather some materials. You will want branches to reinforce your temporary structure from the inside and large flat pieces of driftwood, scrap metal or bark to serve as the outside walls. If you are afraid of the whole thing coming down on you, you can secure the materials together at the top with rope. If you are in an area where you can find a cave (this is more likely in mountainous regions, but caves can be found almost anywhere), just make sure it isn't occupied – the last thing you want is to intrude on the home of a bear or big cat.

If you have been hunting and have some hides that need to be put to use, you can always make a tent. Just gather some good, large branches, strip them down (remove bark and offshoots) and build your frame. Realistically, you can build it however you want if you are feeling creative, but the simplest way to do it is with the conical teepee structure. Make sure your frame is posted firmly in the ground and secure it at the top with leather strips or rope. You will need to sew your hides together so that they fit over the whole frame – make sure there is enough space allotted for an opening so folks can get in and out. If you removed the fur from your hides for tanning, they will not be waterproof and will be less insulated. In that case I suggest insulating your shelter with a fur lining around the top and bottom of the structure; this will add a layer of protection from rain and snow as well as keeping the temperature inside fairly constant. Keep in mind, the larger you can make your shelter, the more people it will fit comfortably inside. If it is large enough with a decent sized opening at the top, you can even build a fire inside – just be careful. (Note: Depending on the area, you might find some clumping bamboo or similar plant such as cane; you can replace larger sticks and branches with these.)

Once you have your camp set up, you can get to building a fire. If there is someone in your party who is practiced in this particular art, give them this job and you will save yourself a whole lot of frustration. If you're by yourself, you really should start practicing fire building now. It's a necessary survival skill, and one that *can* be easily learned, but it takes dedication and a lot of practice to perfect it. Start learning now and you will be in a much better position later.

Just as you had to find an ideal spot for your shelter, you need to find a safe place to build your fire. Look for a spot in or near the center of camp (preferably as far away from any trees, bushes or low-hanging branches as you can get it) where the earth is flat and firm. Clear this area of any leaves or plant life and, if available, make a barrier around the area using rocks. Once you have a safe place cleared out, you are ready to build your fire.

Building a fire is not as easy as it sounds. If you have a lighter or matches, you can figure out relatively quickly how to do this, but if you don't then the task will be quite a bit more difficult. No matter how you plan to build your fire, the first task is always the same: gather some small dry twigs (preferably fallen from dead trees), and some dead grass – this is your tinder, the driest, smallest and most flammable stuff – make a little nest out of it and set it aside to go look for some bigger sticks for kindling. You will want to separate your kindling from the smallest and driest to largest and least dry, as this will be the order in which you will introduce new kindling to the fire.

If you are using a flint and magnesium fire-starter, put your tinder nest into the center of the fire pit and, using one of your knives, scrape some magnesium onto the tinder. (Note: magnesium burns very, very fast, you will need a lot in order to catch a spark and make it spread – you might just make a little pile of magnesium shards on top of the little nest.) Once you have created a primary explosive out of your tinder (don't worry, it won't kill you), grab some smaller sticks and build a little teepee above that, making sure there is a small opening so you can get close enough to aim your sparks at the magnesium in the center. Get in close and strike the flint strip quickly with the edge of your knife (similar to how you would strike a match) so that the sparks fly at the magnesium.

If you don't have a fire-starter, you will need to get old-school – leave your tinder nest close at hand, but off to the side for now and go find a couple of dead, dry sticks and strip the bark off them. Make sure one is about the length of your arm and decently thick (about the thickness of one of your fingers). Choose the stick you want to use as your base (you will want something sturdy and thick) and cut a hole into it about the same thickness as the long stick you will be using for friction. On the side of the hole you just made, cut a notch big enough to tightly fit a small piece of dry wood or bark (this will serve as charcoal). Place a flat piece of wood (you can cut it out from something) underneath the hole in your base to close off the bottom and make sure you don't just shove the fire-starter stick into the ground. Take your long stick, the one about the length of your arm, and stand that up in the hole you have cut into the base; you want to pin the base down using your knee or something – don't let it move. Make sure the notch is plugged tight and begin rubbing the stick between your palms – only use your palms, don't go out to the fingers because you can't put as much pressure on the stick with your fingers.

As you are rubbing back and forth, push down hard on the base, your hands will go down as you push, just bring them back up and continue. Try to increase speed and pressure as you go and when you start seeing smoke, keep going for a couple more seconds until the smoke increases a bit. Once you are really smoking, very carefully use a small stick to dislodge the charcoal piece and fold it gently, still smoking, into your little nest of tinder. Be very careful at this point not to get too ahead of yourself and rush things or else you will mess up and have to restart. Once you have the charcoal wrapped lightly in the tinder, hold it up to the air, gently blow into it. If you see more smoke and hear crackling, you are doing it right. Just keep blowing gently until you actually see a bit of flame start up. Once you have a flame in the tinder, you can set it down in the center of the fire pit and start throwing on your dry twigs. Add kindling in order of size and dryness – the drier and smaller things go first. Let them start to catch before putting larger, wetter things in.

There is a very good reason that many cultures in history had a place where the fire was never allowed to go out. Fire is hard to make, especially with limited resources, so don't get cocky, and be very careful when trying to do this. Unless you have built fires in this manner before, you will probably have a whole lot of trouble making this work and most likely you will not be successful right away. That said, if you do fail and end up with blisters and splinters all over your hands from unsuccessful attempts, try to refrain from getting too agitated. If you fail the first couple of attempts, hand the task over to someone else before trying again, otherwise, you will get frustrated and try to force the fire or rush the process which will only yield worse results. Once you do get your fire going, try to keep it that way – take turns with people keeping the fire alive day and night so you always have a cook fire and a source of heat when you need it.

Travel in Groups:

If you are thinking about going it alone, rethink your strategy. The more people you have, the more you can carry; sharing the burden is good because with three or more people, there is room for an extra bag or backpack to hold things like extra food or supplies. This is also good for carrying trade items if you happen to come across other travelers. Further to this point, there is safety in numbers. In a survival situation, you want to stay on your toes – rotate watches at night after setting up camp, you are less likely to be robbed or attacked with a few other people at your back. If you are hitching or train-hopping (both of these are dangerous and illegal in the U.S.), groups of no more than three are ideal; consider car space and the size of hiding places on trains. However, if you are traveling exclusively on foot, you could practically take a whole village with you, though I'd suggest maxing out at five. Remember, more people means more hunters and gatherers, a higher chance that somebody has skills you don't which you or your fellow travelers might need and more people to respond and help in the event of an emergency.

You might also consider traveling with an animal companion – maybe you have a pet you don't want to leave behind, or otherwise, you choose to take an animal along for purposes of practicality. Either way, it is well known that nomads love their animals. That said, you have a few choices when it comes to taking an animal with you. I've met all kinds of travelers but only two kinds of traveling animals – dogs and cats; however, there are definitely more options than that for the practical and creative animal lover.

Ideally, if you have access to pack animals, such as horses, mules or goats, this is one of the better options. Mules and horses are excellent as they can carry a lot of extra weight and, if somebody gets sick or injured and can't walk, they can be thrown over the back of your horse until you can get to a safe place to take care of them. Another advantage to these two animals is they can navigate easily on rough terrain. However, mules and horses are pretty high-maintenance animals, don't overwork or overburden your animals and make damn sure that they are fed and watered (that should go without saying, really). And keep those hooves clean.

Personally, I think a good female pack goat might be better than both of these others as they can carry a fair amount of weight (albeit not quite as much as horses or mules) and a recently pregnant goat can provide milk. Goat milk is better for humans than cow milk and is also a good breast milk substitute for babies if for some reason you have an infant with you. Aside from that, goats are pretty easy-going and fairly low maintenance, as long as they have grazing room and fresh water. They can also more easily navigate through a rough terrain than the larger pack animals (though, as stated, they all have this advantage to an extent).

As useful as pack animals are, dogs are the traveling favorite (and easier to come by than pack animals). If you have a big enough, well-trained and well-behaved dog, you can strap a small saddlebag to it and have it carry some of your lighter-weight stuff, plus its own food. A saddlebag made for a dog will also fit a goat. Be aware, however, that dogs are not pack animals and do not have the same kind of strength or endurance that people do – if you give your dog a saddlebag, don't overburden it. Make sure that your dog is being constantly hydrated and know that you will need to take regular breaks so neither you nor your dog overheats. Perhaps more importantly than this, a good dog is also a good guard if you train it. It can be useful for protection and alerting you to nearby dangers. Keep your dog close and you should be safe. Dogs are also good for hunting if you have the right breed or if you train it accordingly. However, dogs are not carnivores, but omnivores. They need fruits and veggies too. Make sure you know what your dog can and can't have and share your food; this is good for bonding, and eventually you won't have dog food to give it. Dogs can also be taught to hop trains.

Keep in mind that any animal you take with you is subject to be attacked or killed by larger predators. Be wary of this and try to keep as close an eye out as you can if you choose to take animals on the road with you.

Self-defense and hunting:

Keep in mind while going over this section that you can't learn to hunt or make weapons simply by reading about it. Don't expect to be an expert on any of these things after reading this – you will probably remain a beginner at all of these things until you get good at them, which will only happen with practice. Picking up these skills before you need them is essential to survival preparation, so start early and start seriously.

The first thing to understand about self-defense is that nearly everything has the potential to be a weapon. You have knives and everything you can use for hunting is also good for self-defense. That said, weapons are not easy to make and require a lot of practice both with construction and use. You will likely be using more handmade weapons than store-bought ones, as the materials to make them will be more available to you and ammunition is a finite resource.

Perhaps the most popular survivalist weapon choice is the gun. While guns can be good to have, they are woefully high-maintenance and cumbersome when you are on the move all the time and trying to survive. Also, assuming you are trying to survive outside of existing civilizations, any authority figures you might happen across will single you out for having a gun. This is especially true if you are female or a person of color, but still applies to everyone because you have been living in the wild and will look it.

Regarding the high-maintenance nature of guns, if you don't keep your gun well-maintained and cleaned regularly, it will jam on you and what good is that? Further, bullets are finite and in a real survival situation, they are also a huge commodity – other people will want them, which will lead to unnecessary violence and possibly a grievous waste of bullets. Guns are heavy, particularly the heavy caliber rifles - Especially hunting rifles (because you may not want to hunt with a hand gun) and they really only have the one use. While surviving on the road, speed and efficiency is key. You do not want to be tied down to a heavy, bulky weapon; it will not do you any good. Stay small, stay light, and you'll stay alive.

For the most part, proper gun maintenance and use are things which require a bit of training – hunting with a gun (or with anything, really) is not a thing you can just pick up and do; you might hit your target, but if it is not dead the first time, it runs much faster than you, even injured. And while, yes, you can chase after it, but do you know how to follow a wounded animal, what to look for? If you hit the right spot, the animal should be bleeding a lot, follow the blood and it might be dead by the time you reach it – good for you. If you missed, the animal is gone. More importantly than that, guns are extremely loud and will scare off everything within a mile radius, so if you are not successful in your first attempt, the job of hunting will become much harder the longer you are out. Unless you have experience or training with guns or there is someone in your party who does, you don't really have much reason to carry one.

If you still want a high-impact, ranged weapon, you can choose between a crossbow and a bow, instead of a gun. Both of these require a good deal of skill, but if you pick one, a compound bow is ideal, and you can, and should, get started training with it now, as early as possible. Crossbows are pretty cool and if you know how to use them, they are great, but you run into the same weight and maintenance problems with these that you do with guns. A compound bow is the best of your ranged options as it is light-weight, fairly compact and made in such a way so that it requires less strength to shoot while maintaining the high-impact shot you require. Of course, a good bow is still more difficult to use than a gun, though not really by much – so get started early and learn now. All that said, there is still the major drawback of finite ammo to consider. Of course, arrows can be made if you know how to make them; you can choose to learn this as part of your preparation if you like.

One very basic weapon you can make in times of dire need is a spear. All you need is some basic materials. First, make a spear shaft with a long branch by stripping it of bark and offshoots and then find some sharp rocks and turn them into sharper rocks with a bit of sandpaper or a metal file (the latter you might have in your utility knife), and then secure it to your spear shaft with some strips of leather. If you are into whittling, you might even put some designs on your spear shaft. If you are doing that, why not also try to work it down to a good balance so it is useful for hunting or self-defense? A spear should be balanced more toward the front because that is where all of the weight is. Depending on the weight of your spearhead, about three quarters of the way up from the back end of the shaft would be ideal. When hunting, the balance point of the spear is where you hold it to get the best distance. Hold the spear lightly when throwing (just firmly enough to keep your grip), the foot opposite your spear hand in front, pointed toward prey, spear hand all the way back, body side-face and twist with the throw. Keep in mind that spear hunting is illegal in several countries, so be aware that this is only for survival situations. Also, don't expect a huge distance with a spear throw, this kind of hunting involves getting pretty close to your quarry before you get noticed and run it off. Spears are also good for fishing, though your net might be easier.

Another option for hunting in a survival situation is trapping. This is probably the most practical way to hunt if you are surviving with what you can carry on your back. Trapping requires a lot of skill and resourcefulness – keep an eye out for the movements of nearby animals and be aware of your surroundings. This is a skill you should be learning now, as it will take some time to practice and really perfect your trapping methods. According to Winyan Staz, "unless you take the time to know your quarry you won't catch much. Watch for well used paths, fresh scat and know the times they move along those paths." Hunting and trapping require tactical thinking, an understanding of your surroundings and a familiarity with your quarry. You can't just set traps anywhere, they need to be set in places where you know the animals will be going regularly for food, water, or whatever might attract them. Once you have set your traps, check them every day to make sure nothing else gets to your food before you do or otherwise to keep the animal from suffering needlessly.

There are two classic traps you can make with nothing and improvise as needed (so long as you don't forget the actual physics behind them): the snare and the figure-four deadfall. Staz suggests that "you can make snares out of cordage, shoelaces, light weight wire (best) or things like string, yarn, ropes, etc." Snares are wicked simple and useful for catching small prey (like rabbits, squirrels or very young deer) and you can make them from practically nothing. What you want is your rope or shoelaces, some sticks and a nearby sapling (or large rock to use as a counterweight). You need two sticks of about the same size that have a sharp hook shape. These should be sturdy, because you will need to hammer them into the ground (use a rock). You will need another long, straight stick to lay underneath these two hooks and another that you will stick in the ground maybe a foot or less away from your hooks. Take your shoelaces or rope and tie one end to the sapling, you will want to bend that little tree over the trap to get the leverage you need for this spring snare to work. Take your shoelaces/rope down to where that long stick is under the hooks and find the place where you have the most tension before securing this part using a small piece of wood (about an inch long) tied to the shoelace and snug under the stick

What should happen: the tension will hold the stick off the ground and fasten it into your hooks. Now, you will make a slipknot with the end of your string (shoelace, rope, whatever) and lay that out, using small sticks as stakes to hold it open (not tight, just open). Next, just take one more stick, the last piece of your trigger system, to run down the middle, fixed between the first stake you put down (across from your two hooks) and your hooked stick. Secure your trigger sticks together by creating notches in them to hold them together.

The figure-4 deadfall is a bit simpler and it comes right out of Wile-E Coyote's book of tricks. To build this, get three sticks and some bait, make sure your sticks are big and strong enough to hold up the log or rock.

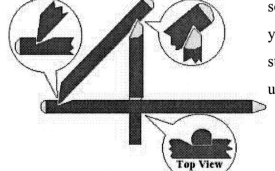

Make some notches in the sticks so they can be finagled into a number 4, as shown in the diagram on the left. Your diagonal stick will be the longest; this is the one that holds the weight of your deadfall. It will be balanced in place by the vertical and horizontal sticks. The horizontal stick rests on a notch near the bottom of the vertical stick and the end pokes inward toward the underneath of your deadfall – this is the actual trigger mechanism. Bait your trigger point and leave the trap, check it daily.

When checking your traps, if you find an animal and it is not dead, kill it by slitting the throat. This is good because it is quick – no reason for the animal to suffer needlessly – and it will bleed out faster as well. Once this is done, you can move on to field dressing the animal you have caught. It is dirty business, so if you have some good gloves, wear them (this isn't totally necessary, but some people prefer to keep their hands clean).

Field dressing is basically just removing the guts. In the interest of not letting things go to waste, there are organs that are edible, such as the heart and liver, but if you are not accustomed to that taste, I'm sure your dog (if you have one) would appreciate a nice snack. To begin the field dressing process, make an incision beginning below the diaphragm (lower part of the chest) and ending down near the genitals. If preferable, you can start by taking a strip of skin first instead of making a full incision, this will clear the area of hair, open it up some more and allow you to get genitals out of the way first. When making your incision, be careful not to cut too deep or you will nick the bowels and that is a stench you won't soon forget. Once you get to the organs, disconnect them from the diaphragm first (careful not to nick the stomach), then get in and cut away the trachea and esophagus. Finish with the rest of the connective tissue and pull those guts out. Remove the head and hang your animal upside-down from a tree to let it bleed out before you skin it. Hanging it with the legs apart will make skinning easier.

Once your animal is bled out, you can skin it - separate the muscle tissue from the hide – that is what the skinning knife is for so make sure it is sharp. Start with the inside of the back legs just below the knee joint (from your upside-down point of view). Be careful not to cut into a tendon or the leg will collapse and make your job harder. Work your way down from the knee toward the pelvic region and just keep working until both the thighs and pelvic region are nice and stripped. From there, you can almost just pull the skin right off, cutting out anything that might give resistance in the process until you get to the forelegs at which point, again, you will be starting on the inside of the leg and working down to release the hide from the chest and neck area. Now, with the skin off and the innards out, you have access to meat and bone. Cut the meat off, separate and clean the bones. Remove the forelegs at the shoulder joint. Cut the ribs away from the rest of the body. Cut excess meat and fat from the outer ribs. Go ahead and throw those ribs over a fire, this work makes you hungry. Remove the back legs at the hip joint. This might be tough because you are cutting out the cartilage at the joint, so make sure your knife is sharp as it can be. Once your meat is separated, carve what's left off the spine and remove the tendons from the legs (they are not tasty, but a dog might like them if you have one). You can carve the meat from the rest of the bones if you want, but it is unneeded.

Once you have your meat, you need to cure and dehydrate it so that it can be preserved. First, trim away all the fat you can and save it (use it to make grease for cooking). Cut your meat up into strips and rub it down well with salt and herbs, seal it up (wrap it securely with leaves or something), for an hour or two. Boil your marinated meat for 5-10 minutes to sanitize it. It can now be dehydrated by smoking. Gather some good wood; maple, mesquite or hickory if available and start a fire, one that will make a lot of smoke (pine needles help with this). Hang your meat strips over the fire and let the heat cook them and the smoke cure them. It will toughen as it dries, and once fully dehydrated will be protected against bacteria. Dehydrated meat (or jerky) is great for traveling because it is lighter than other meat and doesn't require refrigeration.

While you are letting the meat smoke, you can get to tanning the newly obtained hide. One great and easy way to do this is brain tanning. Brain tanning will be how you keep a supply of leather strips, shoelaces, clothing, bags, patches, potholders or gloves. According to braintan.com, "you can make soft, washable leather with emulsified oils and wood smoke. This is commonly known as brain, smoke or Indian tanning. Animal brains are traditionally used as the source of emulsified oils, hence the name, but you can also use eggs or a mixture of soap and oil." Emulsified oils can be made by combining warm water with the brains of the animal you have caught. To begin the tanning process, take what bones you have, making sure they are clean – these can be sharpened and used as pegs to peg down your hide. You can also make a tanning rack with some thick branches if you don't have a flat surface to stretch the hide out on. Just poke some holes around the edges of the hide and tie it tight to the rack. Use a knife to scrape off any excess meat and fat that might still be clinging to the flesh side of your hide.

You can choose whether or not to remove the fur and grain from the hide, depending on your need. You will need to dry the hide by applying a layer of salt to the flesh side once it is cleaned, roll it up and let it sit for a day or two somewhere dry, clean off the old salt, apply new salt and do it all over again to make certain that all the moisture is removed from the hide. Don't be stingy with your salt, and don't just throw it on and roll up, really rub it into the hide or you won't get the full effect. The hide is done when it is tough and dried out rawhide.

While you are drying out the hide, go ahead and prepare the brain. Making three incisions at the top of the head, in the shape of a triangle, you should be able to access the brain matter. Use a spoon or just shake it out. You can mash it up into a raw brain soup to make this easier and mix it with about half a gallon of boiling water to kill bacteria. Warm brain will absorb into your hide more quickly than if it is cold. Let your brain water cool until you can stick a hand all the way to the bottom of your container without burning yourself. Work the dried out hide into the brain water mixture and leave it there to absorb the oils. You can tell where the hide has or has not fully absorbed the mixture by its texture – it will become noticeably softer and lighter in color.

You will need to do more than just hunt for food – despite what some folks may think, people require much more than just meat in order to get the nutrition we require. Diet is important to survival – you can eat all you want, but if you don't get the nutrients you need, you will be malnourished and it could mean your life. However, foraging for edible plant life is different for every bio-region. As already stated, you will need some local field guides and familiarize yourself with local edible plants growing naturally in your region if you don't want to accidentally poison yourself.

There are some foods you will find in multiple regions, including berries. You must be careful with these, as many berries are poisonous, but some of the more common edible ones are easily recognizable. For example, blackberries are an extremely invasive species. They grow in temperate areas and you can find them almost anywhere in the US. You can find wild blackberry patches growing in the spring and into the middle of the summer. Blueberries, strawberries and raspberries grow in temperate, sunny places. They like water, so they grow well in warmer, rainy regions during the summer months as well. Harvest season for these berries is nearer the end of the summer season.

If you come across some berries that you don't recognize and you have a few hours on your hands, here is a process to follow in order to determine whether or not they are poisonous:

- First, take one and crush it between two fingers. Rub them together. Wait about 45 minutes to an hour.

- If nothing happens, scrape a bit of skin (don't flay yourself, just use your nails), rub the berry juice in, wait.

- Still nothing? Put the berry to your lips, crushing out the juices. Wait.

- If nothing has happened yet, taste the berry and wait again.

- After several hours, you have determined the berry is good to eat if no reactions occur through exposure.

- Eat one berry and wait again just to be sure and if you feel nothing, you can eat more of them, but slowly and cautiously.

- If at any time during this test, you feel or see any kind of reaction from the berry's juices, put it down and walk away.

- If you are starving or don't have hours to spend, leave the berries alone for now and check your traps; who knows? Maybe you will find some blackberries.

As fruits are an excellent way to combat scurvy, I suggest you eat a lot of them. However, finding good fruits in the wild may not prove especially easy considering lots of fruit trees in North America (especially the US) are not indigenous. This includes oranges, kumquats and possibly apples, making them difficult if not impossible to find in the wild. Beyond that, since fruits are such a popular commodity, their production is pretty heavily regulated; however, if you are willing to do some urban foraging, most popular fruit trees can be found in backyards and orchards so if you are looking for fruits, find some abandoned houses or orchards nearby, if available.

There are also a variety of different vegetables that can be found in the wild in some form or another, including potatoes, wild yam, asparagus, kale, rhubarb and several others, but these are less nutritionally important than tree nuts. Tree nuts are some of the most important foods you can depend on in a survival situation. To remove the shells from tree nuts, you can use two rocks or your mortar and pestle. Some easier shells can just be cracked with your teeth. Unless you have allergies (in which case, the nomad survival strategy may not work so well for you), nuts are an excellent source of protein and good fats (Omega-3 or -6 fatty acids, especially). They will keep your energy high and your appetite sated on surprisingly little. Pine nuts from any pine tree anywhere in North America (Pine pollen can also be used in teas) are delicious and will energize you. Walnuts are also fantastic, but almonds are even better because they are higher than most other nuts in protein and fatty acids and can be crushed up with your mortar and pestle – just add some water and you will have almond milk (if you have some honey, which we'll get to harvesting later, you can even sweeten it). Don't scoff at almond milk, it is creamy with a slight nutty flavor and aside from being delicious, it will keep you well nourished. You might also find cashews, pecans, macadamia nuts, hazelnuts, chestnuts, etc. You get the idea. Nuts are good for you and there are millions of different kinds. Some are better than others, but in general, collect tree nuts and eat them (unless you are allergic).

One tree nut that the true survivor should never ignore is the acorn. A pound of acorns is roughly 2,000 calories and, though they are bland, they will keep you going. Simply collect acorns, shell them and you can mash them up with your mortar and pestle to make acorn paste. You start this process after shelling them by cooking the nuts in oil (or fat grease) for a few minutes to soften them and then crush them up until they make a fine paste. Any nuts can be turned into a paste in this manner, which can be used for making pancakes or just to be eaten. Make sure not to confuse buckeyes or red horse chestnuts with acorns as they are in the same genus as oaks and their fruits come in similar capsules. According to many experts, there is much argument over whether or not buckeyes and red horse chestnuts are toxic. Apparently, the "green seeds/husks are more toxic" Proceed with caution.

As stated in numerous manuals, these nuts are rumored to be toxic to horses and livestock and may be fatally toxic to toddlers. They have been reported to cause upset stomach or muscle spasms in cases of overdose. However, Juliette de Bairacli Levy, the grand dame of veterinary herbalogy, states that the Horse Chestnut's name was derived from how horses consumed large quantities of these fruits. Also, it was observed that horses showed improvement in respiratory conditions after eating the nuts. Juliette goes on to tell how gypsies and Spanish peasants used the nuts as feed. The bitter taste is often neutralized by grinding the nuts to a powder and then treating with a lime/water solution, washing, and then heating the meal. In this way a highly nutritious starch is produced in Europe. Ms. Levy advises feeding it as a general tonic, which particularly strengthens the pulmonary apparatus. She feeds 2-3 handfuls of prepared chestnuts daily." It seems that buckeyes or red horse chestnuts can be dried and eaten if cooked and prepared (just to be safe). Just don't overdose or you may become ill.

Last but not least, you might come across some peanuts if you look hard enough. If you find some peanuts, either growing wild or planted deliberately, go ahead and take them. They are delicious, and almost as good for you as almonds. Almost.

Just because you are surviving on whatever you can find doesn't mean you can't have some sweets – if you are brave, well prepared and allergy free, you can harvest some wild honey. If you do plan on doing this, add a mason jar or two to your list of things to pack so you can store your honey somewhere. You can use honey as part of your meat curing marinade, or you can make some mead with it. Aside from that, you might also end up with some beeswax, which can be used for all kinds of things. If you have some good gloves (perhaps made from some leather you cured yourself), wear them. You will also want to protect your face with a net. Now, in order to harvest honey from beehive in the wild, you first need to find out where one is. If you find an area with lots of flowering plants, it is likely that you will find some bees there too. Make sure these are honeybees, don't confuse them with wasps or another kind of bee that doesn't make honey. If you do find one, follow it around until you find the hive. This will usually be in a crevice inside of a tree or something. If you see a bunch of bees around, flying in and out, you have found the beehive.

Now, you will want to distract the bees so you can steal their honey (not all of it, you won't need that much). For this, smoke will work. You can make a lot of smoke by burning Spanish moss or pine needles. Light some of those up and waft the smoke into the hive, this will make the bees think there is a fire nearby and they will respond by gorging themselves on honey. While they are gorging, check to see if you can figure out which one's the queen. She'll be bigger than the rest and won't be able to fly. Most of the hive will stay near her. The better honey is farther away from the brood (where the queen is). The brood honey is called "dirty honey" and has more pollen and dirt and such in it. (Note: dirty honey is ideal for making mead, but not as good for eating as the "pure honey"). Once the bees are distracted, they won't even notice you taking some honey so just grab a good knife (doesn't need to be huge, this could be a pocketknife as long as it is sharp) and cut off a piece of honeycomb. There may be bee larvae mixed inside of your comb, these are full of protein and okay to eat. Remember, just because the bees are distracted doesn't mean you won't get stung a few times, but if you do it right, you shouldn't get swarmed. Be careful – too many stings even for someone who isn't allergic can be fatal. Next, just take your honeycomb back to camp and contain it in something; leave it there for a few hours and let the honey ooze out.

You will also need herbs and mushrooms for food and medicinal purposes, but these, more than anything else, are incredibly numerous and unique. Depending on your region, the types of mushrooms and herbs you find might change – there are entirely too many different species with too many toxic look-alikes to give any proper introduction to this type of foraging. That said, going into the wild with no knowledge whatsoever of the herbs and mushrooms around can be incredibly hazardous to your health. Part of preparation should be to familiarize yourself with as many of the plants and animals in your specific bio-region as you can – this is especially important for wild herbs and mushrooms. I can't stress the need for field guides enough – one good guide for mushrooms is the Smithsonian Handbook for mushrooms; it covers every kind you might find growing in the wild with photos for reference and very specific detail to help with identification.

Conclusion:

As we have seen, there are many considerations to take in when you start thinking about Mobile Survival. The most important thing to remember about survival is resourcefulness. Use what you have around you and pay attention to the environment you are in. It is important not to resign yourself to solitude and mistrust in situations like this as well – you never know when you will need help and have to rely on strangers. Traveling in groups is the best thing you can do for safety and security, particularly if your band of nomads is made up of people with diverse skills – the more people with you who know how to do things needed for survival, the more likely you are to actually survive.

As part of your preparation, extend your research beyond this. That doesn't just mean take classes and read more survival guides – go out and explore. Get to know your environment by being in it, participating in it and becoming a part of it. Read books about your particular environment. Learn the flora and fauna. Going mobile after a world-changing event can mean the difference between survival and demise. Being a Nomad Prepper won't work for every person, in every situation, but if it is an option for you and your family, it is one that you should seriously consider. Being mobile provides the benefits of increasing your food supply, staying safe and unpredictable, and being able to discover safer areas or finding help of some sort in another location. It's not always going to be easy, but it can be done. Practice your survival skills – as with most things in life, practice makes perfect. This is the best thing you can do to prepare for going mobile after any life-changing situation, and for keeping you and your family safe.

Prepping with Children: A Family Survival Guide

Introduction

We live in a time of uncertainty. At any moment, we could face a drastic event that could change our lives as we know them. It could be something produced by Mother Nature, such as a hurricane, an earthquake, a wildfire or a tsunami. Or it could be an issue created by our government, such as economic collapse, a military coup, or civil unrest. Other dangers that could end life as we know it are widespread medical emergencies, such as an outbreak of a new fast spreading disease or the return of an old, slightly-changed menace like smallpox. The danger could even be from something as simple as a power grid failure, or as complex a terrorist attack. The list of possibilities is exhausting. Preparing for any number of these events can be too. Even more so when you have children. There are a lot of situations to teach your children to be ready for, but in the end, prepping with children will rely on the same principles as teaching your children anything: patience, repetition, and familiarity. Children are not going to always understand what you're trying to teach them or why it's critically important for them to learn, but prepping and survival skills are all valuable skills to teach them, no matter what type of event you are preparing for.

It would be impossible to be prepared for every possibility and every consequence of each event, but prepping is done in order to make your life sustainable and as comfortable as possible if life as we know it ceases, even temporarily. This is particularly true if you are prepping not only for yourself, but for an entire family as well. You'll want to do everything within your power to ensure the survival of you and your family, and if your children are knowledgeable about prepping, it will make survival much more likely. Prepping as a parent may mean that you are just adding a few extra supplies to your stash, but that would be the most basic solution, and it really should be much more than that. It is a complicated area, ranging from what you should tell your children about the situation, to what you choose to shield them from and how you prepare them for the worst, while teaching them to hope and also prepare for the best.

Life as a parent takes on a whole new meaning, with or without a doomsday scenario. When a child comes into your life, the level of responsibility that you have explodes by multitudes. Life as a prepping parent creates even more responsibilities, more detailed planning, and extra tasks for everyone involved. There are many extra challenges that parents who prep must face. Of course, there are the obvious adjustments to a disaster plan, like planning to have more food and room in your shelter, but there are also many more nuanced things to take into account if you are prepping with children. You must plan for their safety, mental health and preparedness. You have to figure out the best way to explain disaster preparedness to your children without creating unnecessary fear in them. You will also face extra prepping tasks, factoring in the extra supplies your children will need for their safety and comfort. You will have to teach your children a different level of responsibility and skills that other parents may not be teaching their children.

Although being a parent prepper is not an easy role, it should be very rewarding knowing that your children are more likely to be safe in a disaster situation and more prepared to deal with any aftermath of a catastrophic event, whether or not you will still be around. Even if we are lucky enough to never face a catastrophic event, the skills they learn as children preppers can serve them well as they continue in life. A well-prepared parent can make prepping an enjoyable and educational experience for their children, and create many bonding experiences as a family that you and your children can cherish for years to come.

Why We Prep

One of the hardest things for a parent to tackle is exactly how to tell your children *why* you are prepping. If you have been prepping since before they were born, or before they were old enough to form lasting memories of minor situations (about three or four years of age), then they probably don't question what you do in terms of preparation. Since it has always been a part of their lives, they accept it as a normal family activity. They probably assume that all families prep. This can drastically change when your child reaches the age when they have sleepovers or play dates at friends' houses, or if you don't start prepping until they are a few years older. If they go into homes of people who do not prep, or have non-prepping friends over, then they will realize that their family is different from their friends. It's possible that in another family's home your child wouldn't notice one way or the other; it is more likely to be an issue when other children visit your home. Although, the topic may never come up if the visiting children do not notice your preparations or if you do not allow the children into your storage area/bunker. However, this situation creates a great opportunity to talk to your children about why and how you prep and why others may not be prepared for catastrophic events. If one of your children's friends ask about your preparations when visiting your home, you should keep the answer simple so as to not create unnecessary concern for the visiting child.

Another reason to keep it brief and act nonchalant about it is if you do not want news of your preparations to spread through the neighborhood. If you are new to prepping, sit down with your family and discuss why you have decided to now join the prepping world and why you feel it is important to your family. Explain to you children why you want them to learn certain skills. Your children may have questions you cannot answer, but do your best to inform, educate, and allay their fears.

When you explain to your children your reasons for prepping, keep in mind that you do not want to create fear in your children. Keep things simple in terms of scenarios. Children have very vivid imaginations and any scenario you present could create a whole new world of worry and concern for your child. The fact that you are a prepper should not lead to you child having nightmares about people breaking into your house to steal your well-planned stores of food, supplies and weapons. The fact that you have a stockpile and are prepared should create a feeling of security for your children. People who are prepared really are doing it because they love their families and want to protect them. As long as you can get your children to understand that, it should alleviate any fears they have. Keep the dialogue open between you and your children about prepping. If they have questions about why you do certain things, be sure to take the time to explain it to them in terms that they can understand.

Make Prepping Fun

It is also important to take into account your children's mental well-being as part of your prepping, before, during and after a catastrophic event. While you are gathering items for your safe zone, or bunker, make sure you include items that will help occupy your children's minds. This might include some board games, cards, or age appropriate books. If the day comes that you have to stay in your shelter for two or three days, you will want to keep the children occupied. Time seems to pass much more quickly when you have a task or something else to keep your mind busy. If they are busy, they have less time to dwell on whatever situation is taking place outside of your safety zone. A fun game or book will also help take their mind off of things.

As part of preparing your children, make sure that you limit their electronic entertainment, such as computers, cell phones, and handheld gaming devices. If your kids are used to being in constant contact with their friends via computers and cell phones then they are suddenly cut off from the outside world, it is going to make their time in a shelter more difficult. Handheld gaming devices tend to use a lot of power (or batteries), and are not very practical in a survival situation. Since these games are not a necessity, make sure your kids are not going to be stressed by having to temporarily give these items up.

Another idea to keep your children's hands and minds busy is to give the children tasks or chores. It is great that they have something constructive to concentrate on, instead of just sitting around while you do all of the work or important things. This can be helpful to the children as well as yourself. Busy minds have less time to worry. You will get some extra help and the children will feel useful.

As a parent prepper, you must decide what you feel are important skills and knowledge for your child to have when doomsday, or any major event, comes. Prioritize the skills, so you do not overload your child with too much knowledge at once. Start with the most important, but basic items. Remember, most of the skills you teach your children have to be practiced or reviewed occasionally in order for them to keep their abilities and knowledge sharp. When you think about what skills you should be teaching your children, an easy way to approach it is to think about the skills a pioneer would have to have. The pioneers always focused on the four main survival needs: water, fire, shelter and food. Some of the basic survival skills they mastered were how to kill and cook a small animal, how to start and maintain a fire, how to build a basic shelter, how to sew clothes and repair broken goods, how to find safe drinking water, how to grow food, or forage for food, and how to store food when you finally had some. There are many more skills that will help your children in today's world, but it is a great starting point for many families. Some of your choices will be based on your living situation. If you live in a large city, fishing and hunting would probably be lower on your priority list than teaching your kids how to barter and socialize properly. Depending on your own skill level, you may not have even tackled or mastered some of the skills you feel are a high priority. If that's the case, learn them together as a family: you'll all learn vital skills and you'll grow closer as a result of having learned those skills together.

Another tip for making prepping part of everyday life: When preparing your safety zone or bunker, create a small library of manuals and books. It can create a sense of safety knowing all of the knowledge your family needs to survive will be available to them, night or day. It should include a medical book, a mechanical book, basic survival book, a book about preserving food, edible food book and a medicinal herb book. There are many more that would be suitable, but it is a personal choice as to your priorities, and the amount of space you can devote to your library of survival knowledge.

Some things your children will need to know how to do without taking the time to research, or if your family has left your shelter for another secure location, you may not have access to your books and resources anymore. So although the library is helpful, you and you your children may not be able to get to it, or may not have the time to research something if immediate action is required. In the world today, we are used to being able to look up anything in a matter of seconds on the Internet; this means of instant information will more than likely be a no go during a crisis, when power and the Internet stop functioning. Teach your children how to use the index of a book to more quickly access the necessary information they are seeking, and use some of your prep time to read portions of these books with your children. This will get them introduced to the topics, give them a sense of security to know where they can find information, and help you grow closer through the shared experience.

Life-Long Skills

The skills you teach your children as part of your preparations can be skills they enjoy and use for the rest of their lives. One of the easiest ways to introduce some basic survival skills is through camping. Camping teaches kids to work together as a family unit. It also teaches them to live without some of the modern conveniences that many of us have grown accustomed to. Camping should not be a one-time trial run at basic survival. Introduce camping as a regular, fun family activity. Each time you take your children camping you can try to add a new skill to their repertoire, and give them more practice at the skills they have already learned. Maybe through your conversations with your children, they will come up with a task they feel is crucial to your family's survival that you have not yet mastered or had not thought of. If they are old enough, let them research the skill and then teach it to the rest of the family. This is a great way to make your children an active prepping team member.

One of the critical skills they can learn while camping is how to make a fire. The first step in teaching about fire is educating them on where a good location for a fire is. Show them how far away from the tent or a building they should be. Explain to them why they should look up for low, overhanging branches before picking a spot. The next step would be to show them how to create a fire pit to help control the fire.

You can teach them several ways to start a fire without using matches. Some of the more common methods that people teach are flint, friction bow, and magnifying glass (or lens). Before you go camping, give the kids a chance to do some research on starting a fire without matches. There are so many ways, let them pick one and try it while you are camping. There are a lot of videos online that can help instruct your children so they have a better understanding when you let them make their first attempts. Forewarn them that starting fire is not easy. Let them practice under your supervision. This is also when you should be teaching them about fire safety. You can even make a game out of fire starting techniques; if you have children close in age, they can compete to see who can start their fire first. Friendly competition can make the experience a little more light hearted than concentrating on the negative reasons that it is imperative that your children learn skills such as this.

Once they get the fire going, you can teach them to cook some basic foods over an open fire. Camping is also a great opportunity to teach your children all about food safety. Your children should be able to identify foods that are perishable and nonperishable. Teach them how to keep perishables edible as long as possible. They should know how to open a can of food with or without a can opener. If you don't know how to open a can without a can opener, this is an opportunity for you to learn along with your children. Along with food safety, teach your children about edible and inedible plants. It is important for your children to be able to identify a few safe plants that could sustain them for a short period of time. This should include not only greens, but nuts and berries too.

Water is another basic element that is vital that your children are well educated about. It is important that you teach them to find drinkable water, how to identify if water is drinkable and how to filter and boil water to make it drinkable. A great family project is to build a simple water filter. Make sure your children are aware of the dangers of drinking water that is not suitable for consumption. Also teach them to not go to the bathroom near the fresh water source when outdoors. Explain how water can become contaminated, and that several things can help keep your water supply drinkable.

When you take your kids camping, you can teach them the basics of building a basic shelter to keep them out of the weather. It is great that they know how to efficiently put up a tent, but they should know how to create shelter out of natural resources if the need should arise. It is also great to teach them how to build a camouflage shelter to keep others from finding them if the situation should arise that they need to hide from other people. Take this opportunity to explain to them why they may need to hide from other people, and when to make themselves known. Some families employ a safe word, and even a stay-hidden code word. It may or may not be something you want to teach your children, but it is something to think about. Sometimes when adults are in a confrontation, it might be a useful tool to have to use the code word to let your children know that it is not safe to let their presence be known.

The great outdoors gives your children the opportunity to learn so many skills. You could never teach them all in one camping trip. Sometimes an overnight stay isn't needed. Head to a local state park and take your kids hiking. It will not only encourage physical fitness, but you can teach them how to navigate in the woods with a compass and without a compass, using clues from Mother Nature. Educate them on the following trails, and when they should avoid trails. Tracking is another survival skill you should teach them. It can help them avoid predators and to identify the tracks of small edible game. Being able to identify animals by their tracks is an important outdoor skill for their safety as well as a food source.

Fishing is another skill that many people can learn while they are camping or even during a day visiting a lake. You should teach your child not only to fish with a store bought pole, but how to catch fish without a pole. They are many options on ways to catch fish, including with a traditional pole, with nets, with spears, or even with your bare hands. Your children's confidence will soar when they fashion their own pole and catch their first fish, build a net to scoop the fish up out of the water, or build a fish trap. The look on their face when they peek into their fish trap and see a fish is a priceless moment, and one they will never forget. In addition to catching the fish, proper fish deboning and cleaning is a necessary part of the process for children to learn as part of their new skill. Fish is also a great food to teach children to cook over an open fire. They can learn to cook it in a pan or in chunks on stick, depending on the type of fish, and what cooking utensils you have available. All in all, fishing, and it's accompanying activities, are a great way to get your children interested in learning prepping and survivalist techniques, and there is a wide range of skills you can teach them along the way.

Some basic outdoor survival skills can also be taught in your own backyard without going camping. Teach your children to look up into the sky to find out many things. Direction they are headed, estimating the time of day, guessing which type of whether is coming. The sky provides clues to all of these, including the time of day, incoming weather and directions. They can even make a sundial, although it would not be ranking high on the scale of necessary skills to have in a survival situation, it may still be fun for the children and get them interested in learning more. What better way to spend a family evening that snuggled up in your backyard looking at the constellations?

Your own backyard can also be the location for food sources your children learn to create. A garden will provide your family with healthy foods and numerous teaching opportunities. Gardens can be a learning center for your children. Teach them how to properly plan and plant a garden. Which seeds to use depending on where you live and the climate. Which food is easiest to grow (and thus, more useful in a survival situation) versus those that are too fragile or finicky to waste time on in a prepping scenario. Gardens help families become self-sufficient and to rely on outside sources of food less and less. This is extremely important in a survival situation, so the sooner your children learn to feed themselves with homegrown food, the better off they'll be. Gardening not only teaches your children how to provide for their family, but it teaches them about plants, biology, and responsibility. Show your children how to start a garden from seeds, and they will gain a respect for where their food actually comes from and the work that is required to bring it to their plate. They can even learn to start the seeds indoors. They can also be responsible for weeding and watering the plants. When it is time to harvest the goods, let them help with that. This will teach them responsibilities and help them to feel involved with your family's prepping practices.

After your children have helped you in the garden, they will begin to realize the different amounts of time needed to get from seed to maturity, depending on what is being grown. They will recognize that some food grow more quickly than others. The garden can provide food to eat now or food to be consumed later, so they will need to learn to process the foods or store the foods grown in your garden. One of the processes they can participate is to keep the foods for later consumption by learning canning. Some people with generators or solar powered bunkers have a freezer and supply of frozen foods. If you fall into this category, you can teach your children how to safely freeze vegetables from your garden. This isn't practical for everyone, however, especially if you lose your shelter and find yourself on the road. You can also teach them about the food from your garden that can be stored for long periods of time, such as potatoes. They need to be taught the best place and temperature for storage and how long the food can be stored before it needs to be eaten. You can make this fun for your children by giving them a brand new journal, where they can write down their notes about different food types and best practices for storing or eating. This will help them to feel as though they are in control of their learning, which will inspire them to press on.

Another lesson that must be taught is how to harvest seeds from your current crop in order to continue growing plants year after year. You can also teach your children to extend their growing season by doing things such as interplanting crops, using raised growing beds, and building a cold frame. If you are not fully up-to-speed on these concepts yourself, and you think it makes sense for your family's prepping plans, it would be wise to learn and study these techniques together. You can find many books on farming and even DVD's. Make a monthly day where the family learns something new about farming and you'll all benefit from it.

Since we have been covering survival in an outdoor setting, it would be helpful to mention that there are a few novels geared towards teens that are centered on survival. One survival novel that might strike a chord with your preteens is Hatchet by Gary Paulsen. It is a great novel for preteens to read. It is about a boy who survives a plane crash in the Canadian wilderness alone. He must learn to survive with the few items he has. It can be very inspirational for teens/preteens to read about this boy's struggles and triumphs in the wilderness. Hatchet actually evolved into a series of books, but preteen boys seem to really connect with the first novel of the series. It really relays the point that he needs skills and must rely on himself to survive. Later in the series, he also must help another person that he becomes into contact with through another traumatic event survive in similar circumstances.

There is also a popular series of books that places the female as the hero in the family. She must not only survive herself, but she must help her family survive. It is controversial because it involves killing people for survival and entertainment. It is called the Hunger Games. It is based a bit more on fantasy, but there are still numerous takeaways that young girls and teens will find helpful when thinking about self-sufficiency and the need to fight to stay alive. I suggest reading the book(s) before passing them on to your children, just to make sure you are okay with the content. But keep in mind that books are a great way for children to learn more about prepping and become inspired to start on their own.

Prepping Games

Not everything you teach your kids has to be set up strictly in a teacher/student mode. We all now that children can become bored of "learning" if it's too much of the same. To break up the monotony and introduce some freshness into their prepping, games can be a great way to learn. They can teach skills or help reinforce information that will be helpful later. For example, one fun way to pass time during long car rides is to play games. There are some interesting games you can play while you are in the car that will help teach your children important things without them even realizing that you are prepping them for emergencies.

One such game is the "Friends and Family Quiz". As you are driving, ask you children questions such as, "How is Aunt Suzy your Aunt?" and "What does Uncle Bill do for a living?" Have the children explain how different people are related to them or different facts about those people. This teaches them their family tree, how different people are connected to them, and what skills these people have. This is especially important when it comes to people who could be helpful to your children in an emergency. For instance, they may know "Steve" is a friend of Dad's. But by playing the game, they can learn that "Steve" is a police officer that Dad went to high school with. Later, you can then introduce the idea that some people can be more helpful in certain situations than others. By being a police officer, Steve might be more helpful to your children (in your absence) if they need to leave their home due to some natural disaster evacuation or other event. This game will help children begin thinking of who is in their network, and who would be most helpful in what situation.

Another game you can play is the "What if?" game. Give your kids some basic scenarios and ask them to explain what they would do. It gives them a chance to do some problem solving, while showcasing their knowledge and creativity. It also gives you a chance to give them advice about what can happen because of the choices they make. For instance, say that you give them a scenario where Mom and Dad go to a large city 75 miles away for the day to purchase a new automobile, and while you are gone, our city comes under attack (something similar to the September 11th attacks), school is dismissed and the roads are closed. Then, ask them: In this situation, what would you do? If your child answers something along the lines of they would go home, lock the door and prepare to stay there until you could return home, you can discuss the correct and incorrect points of their plan. You can tell them going home is a good idea, but how would they get home if they find the roads are closed? Or what would they do at home if the doors are all locked? This game can present many different scenarios that can become important teaching moments. Your children are able to formulate plans in a non-stressful situation, while showing you how they think and giving you a space to guide them towards the right answers. This teaches them to think through their plans and think of the possible consequences of their decisions.

On a day when you have some free time, another idea is to take your children and go for a ride in the car or walk around your neighborhood on foot. Let your kids direct you on how to get to emergency contact's homes, or how to get to a safe place (police station, fire house, etc). Let them pick the directions and how you would get there, and you can correct them, or praise them along the way. If something should happen to you, you will want to make sure that your children know the address and directions to family members' homes, and how to tell someone how to take them there.

Alternatively, you can spend a free day or two teaching them how to read a map. This is a skill that will be helpful to them their entire lives, and even more so in a prepper event. Even in a world with GPS on every Smartphone, you children should know how to read a map. Electronic help and satellites can easily become disabled. Let your children know that using a cell phone also lets others track their movements to a certain degree. Depending on a situation, this could be helpful or harmful to their survival. Being able to read a map will be a great survival skill and, if you learn together, most children find it to be a very fun process.

You can also play a lot of other games at home to teach survival skills in a fun way. For instance, hide and seek is a common children's game, but one that can be used as a vital teaching tool. Let your kids play it with you being the seeker, and them trying to hide from you. Then, after you find them, teach them better ways to hide. You can explain why the spot they chose to hide may not be the best choice. Give them different options that they can consider next time. Later, you can let them employ camouflaging techniques to make the game even harder. You may be surprised at how quickly your children become masters at hiding, and this is a skill that will serve them well in any survival satiation.

Rabbit and Fox is another game that can teach survival skills. In this game, both the person acting as the rabbit and the one acting as the fox are blindfolded. The object of the game is for the fox to catch the rabbit only by listening to the rabbit's movements. The rabbit is trying to reach the safety point (a spot determined before play begins). The blindfolds are to simulate the fox hunting the rabbit at night. This game teaches children to use their other senses and to incorporate stealth like movements, as well as how to be aware of your environment at night.

There are other ways you can make playtime into learning experiences as well. For example, as part of outdoor play, teach your children to climb trees. Show them the best trees to climb quickly. Show them the trees that provide the best cover when using them as a hiding place. This can help your child escape a predator or escape detection from people. These are just some of the games you can play with your children that will also serve as great teaching moments. The more you engage with them and the more you involve the entire family, the greater of an impact that any of these games will have. Make these games part of your regular family entertainment, and you'll be instilling survival skills in your children, all while having fun and growing together.

Activities Outside of the Family

Apart from prepping at home or with the entire family, encourage your children to join groups and teams, which will teach them many different types of skills that will be useful throughout their lives. Groups such as the Boy Scouts and the Girl Scouts can teach your kids a lot of outdoor and survival skills. Sports teams are also great for your kids. They help keep them in good physical condition and they teach them how to work as a member of a team. Being a member of a team helps them build relationships with people outside of their family. It helps prepare children by experiencing the disappointment of things not turning out the way you hope or expect, while also increasing their social abilities, which can come in very handy.

At some point, either in group sports or other non-family activities, your children will also probably experience the disappointment of dealing with people who do not act with the group's best interest at heart, but who, rather, act in a selfish manner. Dealing with these types of disappointments and successes helps build your children's character and prepare them for life's trials and tribulations. Bigger disappointments and successes will undoubtedly come later in life, but these early learning sessions will help your children to be better equipped to deal with them. If you are active in your church, youth groups centered around your church can also help your children build connections outside of your immediate family.

Another great "outside of the family" activity: First Aid. You should look into signing up your kids up for a first aid class as soon as they are old enough to take one. This should include basic first aid for wounds and injuries, as well as CPR training. Some of the emergencies you will probably want your children to be able to handle are burns, cuts, sprains, and how to stabilize or deal with trauma. You can also sign them up for more advanced classes that teach more in-depth information about medical emergencies, such as seizures or heart attacks, and a wider class of wounds and injuries. The three most important medical skills that your children can learn for doomsday are treating trauma injuries, stitching wounds and CPR. At the bare minimum, find a class that will teach the basics of these 3, and your children will be better equipped than 95% of the rest, should the need arise.

Speaking of health care and safety: Another simple technique your children can learn that can save someone's life is the Heimlich Maneuver. Depending on your children's age or body size, it may not be a maneuver that they can execute themselves, but in an emergency, they can convey the necessary instructions to another person.

In addition, you should educate your children on your family's specific medical issues. If you have a member that is diabetic, make sure the kids know warning signs of an insulin spike or drop and what to do if there is an issue. They should also know each other's allergies. Make them familiar with the family's prescription and OTC medications. Teach them how to read medical labels, especially dosage charts. If you wish, you can also educate your children (or yourself) on medicinal herbs. There is so much information about medicinal herbs that this would be a situation where your child should learn to research and study the medicinal herb book you should store in your bunker. Knowing about your family's specific medical information will help your children feel connected to the reasons you are prepping, and could prove to be the difference between life or death later on.

If the big event that spurs a meltdown and a need to switch to survival mode is a medical event, such as an outbreak of a new contagious disease or the return of smallpox, make sure your children understand how germs are spread. Teach them to avoid touching their eyes, nose and mouth when they, or anyone close to them, are sick. Make sure they comprehend the importance of hand washing, and how to sanitize items. Medical masks should be part of your medical kit, and you should teach kids how to properly use them. You should also make them aware that if a medical event is the catastrophic event that leads to you implementing your preparations, that they should avoid contact with others outside of your house unless instructed by you to do so, or unless they can determine the others are completely safe.

Vitamins should also be part of your proactive approach to staying healthy before or during a disaster. If food supply is limited in a disaster scenario, your family might not get adequate vitamins and minerals from the food you are eating. In order to combat this, have your family members take vitamins while sheltering. Children should be aware of the dangers of taking too many vitamins and should be educated on how, when, and how many vitamins to take. The gummy vitamins might be easier to get your children to take in the beginning, but in an emergency situation, they might be very tempting to a child to take too many of them, and therefore they would be putting their health at risk. Teach them proper vitamin usage and the importance of vitamins, and they'll have one more tool in their arsenal, should the need arise.

There are a lot of community classes that can benefit your children, whether doomsday comes or not. When they are young, do everything you can to teach your children how to swim. Swimming lessons are available at most YMCA's and health clubs. If these are not an option, you need to teach them yourself, while they are still young. This is a skill that can save their life or someone else's, and it is a skill that is fast on decline in our modern world. If the need arises to evacuate the family's safe area, there may be a time when they have to cross a creek or river to reach safety. They also might be in a situation where they have to swim to escape people or to save someone else. Swimming is one of those things that is much easier for children to pick up and latch onto when they are young, so all efforts should be made to teach this to them at an early age, and to foster their growth as swimmers as they grow up.

Safety and Defense

Self-defense is another type of class you should consider signing your children up for. It could be basic self-defense tactics, like how to escape from someone trying to grab you, to more disciplined martial arts training. Martial arts training takes a lot of time and commitment, so it may not be for everyone, or you may want to start off with the basic self-defense and progress to more finely skilled martial arts. Martial arts include Karate, Taekwondo, and Judo. Self defense will not only give your children the skills to handle situations where they feel endangered; it will also build their self-confidence, since they will feel like they are more capable of taking care of themselves. How much self-defense training you wish to give your children can depend on your personal views and your family situation, but it's safe to say that, at a bare minimum, we would want our children to have a basic knowledge of how to defend themselves, if necessary.

One course that is a necessity if you own firearms is a gun safety course. It is absolutely vital that your children understand how to safely handle a firearm and the dangers of firearms. Some courses simply cover the basics of gun safety and this is okay, to start with. If your child takes the basic gun safety course, consider next enrolling them in a firearm-training course, where they will actually learn to safely load, handle, and shoot a gun. Sometimes this is best left to instructors other than yourself, if you are not fully comfortable with a weapon yet. And sometimes it's best left to someone else, not because you are not a capable marksman or don't handle a gun properly. It's just that sometimes another adult can educate our children in a way that we don't. Being exposed to another teacher is not a bad thing, particularly with something as important as handgun safety. This way your child is learning from two people: their instructor and yourself, and can retain the best parts of both instructions.

The act of shooting a gun on a range is vitally different than simply talking about doing it. The act of firing a weapon can be very powerful in teaching children the true dangers and power of a weapon. And despite other people's opinions of your child handling a weapon, remember that a child trained to properly handle a weapon is a safer child in a doomsday or survival situation. In addition, firearms are not the only weapons you can teach your children to use. There are bows, tasers, crossbows, or knives. If firearms are your first choice as a weapon, take into account your children's ages and maturity if you want to enroll them in a firearm training course. If you wish to teach your children how to use other weapons, like those mentioned above, there are many different courses, both online and in person, that will teach each of those weapons, from basic to advanced.

It's also important to teach your children that many tools can also double as a weapon in a pinch, such as axes, screwdrivers, a box cutter, shovels, and hammers. The act of firing a weapon may be too frightening for some children, and others may never feel comfortable handling a weapon. It is okay for your children to have limitations. You must understand and respect that. They do not need to master every single skill that you would like to teach them, and it is important for you to accept their refusal on some skills. Work with them and their comfort zone to find a method of self-defense and self-protection that works best for them. Nobody knows your children better than you, and it's your job to prepare them while making them feel completely comfortable with their abilities.

If defending your bunker or safe zone is something you plan to train your children to help you do, there are several ways you can practice this. First, you should train your children to patrol the perimeter of your area. This would be your first line of defense against attackers. Teach them how to patrol without being seen by outsiders. Demonstrate how one person patrols a certain area, while another person patrols the adjoining area. These two people need to be in contact via hand signals, physically meeting, or using radios to confirm that the other has not seen any intruders and ensure that they have not been captured or injured by intruders. Teach your children what to look for, in terms of broken perimeters, threats far beyond the perimeter, or just anything that may be out of the ordinary.

To make this training fun and more memorable, some preppers get friends or family to come to their house or shelter to play a basic game of capture the flag (with the flag being placed inside your bunker or at its entrance). Have one team try to breach the perimeter unnoticed, while your children must try to spot the intruders and keep the flag safe. Other preppers have their children practice live fire scenarios by using paintball weapons in place of real firearms, depending on the age of your children. The paintball option is a great practice technique for those who want a more realistic situation, but should be taken with caution and care.

Besides defending the home, you should help your children practice how to escape from your bunker or safe zone if you are attacked. An escape plan should be in place for your home, your safe zone and even your bug out location. Your children should know this escape plan and be able to recite it from memory. Doing a live escape drill every so often will help cement this plan into their minds, and provide a new take on training for it. If you need to escape your home or bunker, you may want to implement your Bug Out plan in this situation, or you may want a different place to meet up after you escape.

Bug Out Plan

Crafting a Bug Out plan is usually one of the first steps preppers take or, if they are completely inexperienced, it is one of the most important steps that people simply skip. A Bug Out Plan involves having a location that you and your family plan to escape to if you need to leave the immediate area, and an idea of how to get to that place. It is a meeting spot for your family somewhere safe, if your current location becomes unstable. Most people prepare a BOB or bug out bag that is filled with a few necessary supplies to sustain you until you can secure more supplies or return to your home. Bug Out Bags are also referred to as PERKs (Personal Emergency Relocation Kits) and GOOD Bags (Get Out Of Dodge).

Some people prepare a bug out bag for each family member, as having their own bag can help children feel more involved and more invested in the prepping plans. A BOB can be as simple as a backpack for a child with a blanket, a comfort item, a bottle of water and a granola bar. For young children, the fact that they have their own bug out bag can make them feel important and give them a sense of security in an uncertain situation. For older children, they can actually help shoulder the burden of the supplies you are taking. If you are bugging out on foot, too many fully-loaded BOB's could be a great strain off of your back. Having your children prepared to carry their own bag makes this much easier. Make sure your children are aware of your bug out location, where the BOB's will be stored, and how quickly to get to the BOB's and start heading towards the bug out location. If something happens and the family is not together when the event takes place, you want your children to know where to meet up with you. This may be the only thing they remember and the only thing that drives them forward.

One bug out location option could simply be to meet at home and bug out together from that point. If the event occurs while you are at work and your children are at school, having a plan to meet up at home first, before anything else, can be an important way to make sure the family sticks together. Another option could be a plan like: Mom picks up the youngest child at daycare; Dad picks up the older children at school - and then the family meets up five miles outside of town at a predetermined location. Children should know where the BOB's are located in your home and which one is theirs. If the emergency arises, you will be rushed and the children can help you gather the BOB or the multiple BOBs and get out of your home quicker.

You should also plan for different scenarios for your bug out plan. Most people do not do exactly the same thing everyday. Children may have play dates at a friend's or be spending the afternoon at the movies with a family member. Have some alternate plans in place in case your bug out location is compromised in the catastrophic event. Some people create another BOB that they keep in their car in case an event would prevent them from returning home to get their BOB. You can try this – or keep one at home, one at the office. There are any number of ways to approach having a BOB and a bug out plan, but the important thing to remember is that ALL of the family should be aware of both parts of the plan, and how to follow it, should the need arise.

Additional Skills

Communication:
Earlier, handheld radios were mentioned as part of a perimeter patrol for security. There are both good and bad points to having handheld radios. If you choose to use radios, that can be a great tool to keep children involved. Make sure your children understand how to use them, the range of the radio, and how to recharge them. On the other hand, you should also teach them that the radios are not a secure method of communication. Other people, maybe desperate people, can hear the transmissions made from one of your handheld radios to the other, and may try to track you or your

family based on those communications. So if you choose to use the radios, please create a shorthand or code that only your family will be able to decipher.

When my children were toddlers and we were getting ready to go somewhere, we would ask the children "Ready, Freddy?" It was a simple, fun rhyme. So our code word on the radio for being in position and ready is simply "Fred". If your child said, "I am Fred" on the radio, someone else would think he was just saying his name. We don't say, "Freddy" because it is too similar to "ready" when heard over the radio. So you don't need to come up with an entirely new language, but think about some phrases that only your family uses or nicknames only you would know. This is often the best way to communicate over the radio. Teach your children not to respond when outsiders try to talk to them over the radio unless instructed to do so by you. The radios really are an invaluable tool, but they have to be used with caution. There may be situations that evolve out of a doomsday event that would make radio usage dangerous. Warn your children that if things get extremely desperate, they may need to go radio silent just to keep others from locating your family based on the range of their radio transmissions.

An alternative to using radios is using signals. Teach your children how to make signals with reflective objects, and using hand signals. Being able to communicate without making a sound could save their lives, and when patrolling around the perimeter of your shelter, it can save some energy by signaling that they are in distress or that they are okay without making physical contact with the other person. It is also another great option in case the radios become inoperable due to lack of power or breakage.

Driving:

Another skill you can teach your children, even if they are not yet of legal driving age, is how to operate a motor vehicle. Your best bet, if you do not have a large property yourself, is to take them to a friend or family member's large property outside of a city, so they have a large area to practice in. Another option is a remote area where you will not encounter any other moving vehicles. Some people may think this skill is unnecessary, but in a situation where you become injured or incapacitated, it could be vital to your survival if your child could drive you to assistance. It also gives your teenage children the ability to leave an unsafe situation if they are not with you when doomsday strikes. This is not suggesting that your child drive on the streets as an unlicensed driver at any point in the normal course of things, but in an emergency, it may be the best choice they have to reach safety or seek assistance.

Think about a Bug Out situation, if you are fleeing to the woods, and there are several heavy gates that have to be opened and then closed. It would be a time saver to have a child who is capable of maneuvering a vehicle through the openings as you opened and closed gates. This is a skill they will learn as a teenager anyway, but even a preteen is capable of operating a vehicle, when necessary. If possible, teach your child to operate both an automatic and a manual transmission vehicle. You may have to exchange vehicles or borrow them at some point, and you won't be picky when that time comes. Teaching them to operate other types of vehicles could be helpful too, such as motorcycles, four-wheelers, and golf-carts. You can easily stress that this skill is only to be used in an emergency situation, and that it is part of the prepping process. Most children can easily understand this distinction and will take on learning to drive as something of great importance.

Sewing:

Sewing, or even basic mending of clothes, should be something your children are taught, whether you are prepping for doomsday or not. Sewing is a skill that seems to fall to the wayside more and more these days. People in today's society seem to feel that clothes are a disposable item. When a piece of clothing rips or has a hem come out, people just toss the clothes into the garbage can and go buy another. It is wasteful, not to mention expensive. Teaching your children the basic stitches to mend clothes will save money, and give them skills that will be very handy. It will make them less likely to be wasteful, and in the event of doomsday, they will be able to keep fix simple tears and keep clothes usable. They should be able to sew on buttons and replace a zipper. Basic sewing skills can also come in handy in altering clothes to fit. If the major event is prolonged, there may need to be alterations to clothing to keep them usable. Adults will probably have some weight loss and children will continue to outgrow their clothes. Just knowing how to release a hem could make the difference between comfortable clothes and uncomfortable clothes.

Just like the pioneers and generations before us knew, scraps of clothes that are no longer usable can be repurposed into something usable, such as scraps of cloth turned into a quilt or tying up shelters, or kitchen rags, or a hundred other things. Some people choose to take prepping to the next level by learning to harvest wool, spin the wool into yarn and then weaving the yarn into fabric. This might be a task you want to teach your children, but it goes beyond the basics for many preppers. At the minimum, your children should know how to sew, to mend hems, to fix rips, and related tasks. This will prove useful after any major prepping event, will give them something to do to keep their minds occupied, and is just a good skill for them to know in general.

When you are preparing your items for your stockpile, you'll want to take into consideration the sizes of your children and the climate you live in. If you live in an area that sees a wide variation of temperatures throughout the year, make sure you store clothes for every season. Make sure you store clothes in different sizes for your children, keeping in mind that you won't know for how long the emergency or survival situation will last. For instance, if you are preparing clothes in the middle of summer, make sure you are putting away a winter coat one size larger than your child is currently wearing. The same thing goes for shoes. Update your stockpile of shoes on a regular basis. It would be unfortunate to have stored a pair of size 4 boots, and then have an event happen a year later and the child needs a pair of size 6 boots. Waterproof boots are a great item to have for children. They are easy to slip off and on in a hurry, but make sure you have comfortable walking shoes in your stockpile for your children too.

Having discussed all of the above survival skills that would be helpful for your child to know, there is no way that those cover everything. There are some simple tasks that you should teach your children that just don't quite fit in with other areas of training. For example, tying knots is a very usable skill, either in a doomsday scenario or in everyday life. A good knot can save you from some big headaches. Some of the basic knots that children should learn are the bowline, clove hitch, taut-line hitch and whipping. Practicing tying knots can be a good pastime for kids when you need to them to have a quiet activity, for instance on a long car ride. As their skills increase, you can add more difficult knots to their repertoire. Or, if your kids like to learn things on their own, they can go online and watch videos on tying knots. They might even teach you a new knot or two. For most knots, they just need a small length of rope to practice with. It's a cheap skill to learn, but one that can prove very valuable in a survival situation.

Another skill that doesn't necessarily fit in another category is making rope from natural materials. It is an easily researchable skill, and a multitude of videos exist online demonstrating how to do it. And the final skill that doesn't really fit in with any of our other categories is candle making. It is definitely a skill that pioneers would have learned, and could be useful to your family if we experience an end to the power supply that was not restored for an extended period of time. Most people think that they will just rely on generators, but even those are a finite source, depending on how much fuel you have.

Personal hygiene is another area that children may have to be reminded to take care of in a doomsday situation. One thing that they cannot slack on is brushing their teeth. If there is an emergency, dental care is going to be hard to come by, and anyone who has ever had a toothache will tell you that it can quickly make you miserable. Dental infections can lead to so many more medical problems down the road, that it is best to do preventative measures everyday to ensure your dental health. Teach children the importance of keeping a healthy, pearly set of whites, and it will be one less thing you will need to worry about in a survival situation.

Besides clean teeth, another priority is making sure we have a clean body; it not only makes people feel better, but if you're clean, you'll be running in top shape. When you are clean, you are more likely to feel energetic and to feel good about a situation. When you are dirty, it can be depressing. It would be a mistake to underestimate the importance of mental health in a survival situation, and staying clean is one small step that can have a huge impact for you and your family. It is best to keep a supply of shampoo, soap and deodorant in your stockpile for this reason. Soap making is a skill you may want to teach your children, or learn for yourself. Some preppers stockpile large amount of personal care items they purchase using sales and coupons. For these preppers, soap making is probably not a skill they would feel they need to teach their children, or the effort is not worth the time investment, and they would rather spend a few bucks to make sure their stocks are full. For families who already try to implement a more self-sufficient lifestyle, it might be a better fitting skill.

Another hygiene item many people purchase is baby (or diaper) wipes. Depending on the age of your children, baby wipes may be a great thing to keep on hand. They take up a relatively small amount of space and can be purchased inexpensively with coupons. They have a fairly long shelf life until they are opened. They can be regenerated if the container dries out before use, just by adding some water to it. They can be used to clean toddlers and young children when a bath is not available. They make great hand cleaners, and are even great for refreshing some the smellier parts of adults. Often overlooked, these wipes can have a wide range of uses and might be worth considering.

Preppers who are females or have female children will also have to take into consideration female hygiene. To prepare, you should have a stockpile of sanitary pads and tampons. They can be multi-purposed in an emergency. Pads are great to use when putting pressure on a bleeding wound. Some people sew flannel pads that are washable and reusable, which were referred to in the paragraph about sewing. They are a great alternative if your supply dwindles or doesn't exist.

Food Prepping

Next to water and shelter, food will be your most pressing concern in a survival situation. Animals are, of course, a great food source, and can be a continual food source, if managed correctly. Two great animals for your children to raise before, during and after a doomsday event are chickens and rabbits. Both take up a relatively small space and are easy to manage. Another benefit of these two animals is that they are commonly allowed within housing areas that have livestock restrictions, even in some big cities, in the case of chickens.

Chickens can be great because they produce eggs for a constant food supply, but by breeding the chickens, you can also get chickens to butcher and consume. The feathers from chickens can be washed and dried, and then later used for stuffing for beds. Eggs are wonderful source of protein and energy, even if you don't use the chicken for meat. These are some of the easiest animals to take care of and to involve children in the care of.

Rabbits breed at a quick rate, so they can make steady food source also. Rabbits are also good because they can forage and eat food that will more than likely be readily available, even in the event of doomsday. In addition to being used for meat, rabbit pelts can be tanned and used for other items such as blankets, clothing, and stuffing for bedding. Also relatively easy to raise, some children may have a harder time, emotionally, raising rabbits to be used for food, but if you explain the reasoning and the necessity of the situation, most children are eager to learn more about animal husbandry.

A third animal to consider, but one that is not allowed in some zoned areas, are goats. Goats are another great small animal for kids to help raise. They require very little upkeep, and are very sturdy, durable animals in most climates. In addition to meat, they can produce drinkable milk. Goat milk is not just good to drink; it can be used to make soaps, lotions and shampoos.

Sometimes you cannot produce enough meat for your family with the livestock you have, or maybe your family desires a wider variety of meat choices. Hunting for small and large game is certainly an option for any survival scenario. Children can be taught to hunt for both large and small game. There are so many methods of trapping and killing game that I won't go into great detail here, but there are some basic things to take into consideration when teaching your children to hunt or trap animals. They should know what types of animals they should be looking for and tracking, and which animals are either not worth the hunt, too risky, or simply don't have enough quality meat. They should also know the typical behavior of the animal, and which of their senses is heightened. You can take children on hunting and camping trips and help them learn how to look for animal tracks or other signs, how to follow an animal trail, and how to hunt and clean an animal.

One of the reasons that children should know about typical animal behavior is that if an animal is acting extremely unusual, it could be either diseased or injured. An animal that is potentially diseased is not suitable for eating. Also, by knowing the typical behavior of some animals, your children will know the animal's strengths and weaknesses. For instance, whitetail deer have strong senses of sight, smell and hearing. This makes them a more difficult animal to kill than, say, a squirrel. Wild turkeys can also be difficult if you are inexperienced, because of their keen eyesight. These types of tricks and tips will be fun for children to learn and will serve them well as they grow into even better hunters.

Another consideration in which animal to hunt is the amount of food the animal will provide or the amount of meat you will have to process. If your family is on the move from one location to another, it would not make sense to hunt a large animal like a deer, when most of the meat would go to waste. On the other hand, if you're staying in one location, a deer would be an excellent animal to hunt, because it can provide an enormous amount of usable meat for it's size. Your children should also be familiar with setting up a trap, and how to do so without trapping or injuring themselves. One of the easiest trapping methods is using a snare wire. More information on traps can be found in many survival books at your local library, or simply online. There are far too many to cover here, and I typical hunt with a rifle or a bow, so I'm not the expert on every type of trap.

Your children also need to know how to properly process and preserve any animals that they hunt. The first step is teaching them to gut the animal. This is not a pleasant process for most children the first time they see it done. But again, it is a great lesson to learn, and becomes easier with each passing time. Not only does it teach about the circle of life, it can be a great anatomy lesson. The decision has to be made of what process is best to preserve the meat. If it is larger game, like deer, they can salt the meat, smoke the meat, or can it. Canned meat is less common than the other two methods, but all of the methods are a means to an end. They provide an edible source of protein to be available for your family at a later date. It is important that your children learn and are aware of the great amounts of effort that go into feeding your family. Everything from tracking an animal, to hunting or trapping, to processing, to cooking, and to storing. Learning all the parts of the process will help children appreciate the work that goes into eating, and will get them thinking about what they need to know to be able to do it themselves.

Other Skills

Mechanical repair is another area that your children can help you with during a survival situation. To prepare them for life after a major disruptive event, they should be able to identify all basic tools such as a hammer, crescent wrench, socket wrench, screwdriver, tape measure, pliers, drill, saw and level. They should know the difference between a Philips and flat screwdriver. They should be able to find a wrench or a socket of a specific size. Teach them to read a measuring tape, and how to use a level. Even if doomsday never comes, they will thank you for this knowledge when they move out into their first apartment or home.

There are some unusual skills that you may want to think about teaching your children, in addition to the above. Now, no one is encouraging you to teach your children to be criminals, but some of these same skills could be very useful to your family post-catastrophe. Of course, you know your children best, so use your judgment when determining whether they are old enough, or mature enough to master some of these skills. They aren't for everyone, but in a survival situation, they can become extremely useful skills to have.

The first such skill is picking locks. Not the first skill that people think of learning. But, it could help you gain access to food and supplies, reach a new location for safety, or even just save you a headache if you lose a key. It is a skill many adults do not know, so you may have to learn it before you can teach it to your children. You never know when it may come in handy though.

The second skill is hotwiring a car. Unlike the movies and television, it's not quite that easy. However, it's certainly not impossible, and could even be very useful in a survival situation. This would be used to start your own vehicle if you lose your keys, need to get your car started in an emergency situation or borrow a family member's car. Or say you're forced out of your shelter and need to flee. Your car is gone. Your neighbors are gone. You see one of their cars still on the street, sitting empty for the past 6 months. Wouldn't you like to know how to get it up and running, as opposed to trying to walk and find freedom?

Another skill is siphoning gas out of a vehicle. If you own more than one vehicle, the time may come when the use of one is a priority over the other and if gas is scarce, siphoning may be the best option. You may have other things that have gas that could service you, like your lawnmower or go-kart. But you need to know how to get that gas out, and back into your car. This is where siphoning comes in handy. I would only teach this one to older children, as it is a bit more dangerous, but no less useful, if you find yourself in a tight spot.

Miscellaneous Skills and Things to Consider
Communication skills, as mentioned above, are another area that your child should master whether it is doomsday or not. By being effective communicators, they will be able to build good relationships, be more effective leaders (if needed), and communicate in an efficient and productive manner. When people communicate effectively, it can save time and persuade people to work together. Part of communication is being able to talk to adults in an adult manner. This can be necessary if your child would end up in a type of confrontation with an adult post-doomsday. Not only that, but good communication skills will serve your child well throughout life.

A child who can communicate as an adult will command more respect. If your child is bartering for items, this will be a necessary skill for them to have; otherwise adults will try to take advantage of the situation and trade unfairly with them. One of the best ways you can teach your children the skill of bartering or trading is by taking them to garage sales or flea markets. Pick a small item and let them haggle for price with adults on their own. It is a confidence booster and puts practice to use with someone outside of the normal group of adults they usually interact with. Part of bargaining or trading is knowing the value of items. A fun exercise to do with your children is to give them scenarios of items you have and items that you need and what would they trade. Obviously, the point of this exercise is to teach them what is necessities and what is not. They will also learn to evaluate what will be valuable to others given certain scenarios. It is a fun game to play for children, and they'll be learning important lessons along the way.

One thing you may overlook when prepping is preserving family photographs. Now, you may be thinking that they are not a necessity but maybe would be nice to have around. The truth is, you do need them. And not just for sentimental reasons (though they are nice for that, as well). If a family member becomes separated from the rest of the family, you would need a photograph to go out and search for them. How else will strangers be able to tell you if they have seen your family member or not? It is handy when making copies of missing posters. Since you are a prepping parent, you know how quickly children change and grow. Try to keep a recent picture of all family members in your shelter. It will not only provide comfort during the dark periods, but can also be extremely helpful, if the need arises.

There are many things you can talk to your children about preparing for, but there is no real way to practice. The best thing we can do is teach our children the skills and personality traits of survival. One important one is perseverance. Hopefully you have taught your children to not easily give up if at first they don't succeed, but again it is something that is taught to your children over a long period of time, and something they will keep learning their entire life. Another one is compassion for others. Compassion is something that we want our children to have, of course, but something that becomes very important in survival mode. We want them to be kind and caring to others, but in the event of doomsday, their compassion has to be kept in check. Although there will be people in need of help, you will not be able to help everyone without compromising your own safety and viability. It is a fine line that you will want to discuss with your children when they reach a level of maturity when they can handle this harsh reality of life after a doomsday event.

One of the best ways you can make the experience of life after a doomsday event better for your kids is to provide them with a sense of normalcy, as much as possible in that situation. Your life may be completely different, but try to set up a new schedule in your new life. If children know that lights are out at 7:30 pm every night, and everyone gets out of bed at 6:00 am, it will provide comfort in the long run by establishing these new rituals and giving them something to rely on each day. Another way to create a sense of normalcy, besides setting a daily schedule, is to explain the new life situation to the best of your ability, and limit their access to scary news reports via Internet, television or radio. Occasionally, let them make a minor decision so that they feel like they have a bit of control in this new environment. It's important that we keep them from becoming completely overwhelmed, or they may just shut down.

If you have a special needs child, you will know what extra steps will be necessary to keep your child safe and comfortable in the event of doomsday. Extra preparations are probably already a part of your everyday life, so you will be able to handle the thought of the extra care you will need in preparing your child. It will be even more important to keep instructions, skills and stress to a manageable level for your child.

Some movies about survival can open up a dialogue with your children about the choices the characters make or what your children would do if they were faced with the same scenario. Or maybe they can just be a great way to spend an evening with your family. Some great survival movies for families include Castaway, Swiss Family Robinson, the Life of Pi, Red Dawn (either version), I Am Legend, War of the World (Tom Cruise edition), 2012, and The Day After Tomorrow. Depending on the age of your children, there are more movies that have somewhat more adult themes to them, but that are no less helpful. They include Zombieland (comedy), the Book of Eli, the Postman, The Grey, Alive, and The Edge. A fun movie about life after an "End of the World" event in the shelter is Blast from the Past. It gives preppers a good laugh about what would happen if they mistakenly went into a shelter for 10 years (or longer) then emerged into society again. Left Behind is another good movie, but it is Christian based so it may not appeal to some preppers.

My Story

One of my first experiences with preparing my family for a major event was making sure we all had an Every Day Carry (EDC) bag. This is a special challenge for a child in public school, as knives and any fire-making tool will get them expelled, but there are many things that they can still have to keep them prepared in an emergency situation. My wife and I gave them a small flashlight, a compass, a map, a few bandanas, balloons, waterproof lipstick in a bright color, crayons (a grease pencil is also an option), a small memo pad or a few sheets of paper, a compact mirror, a 9-volt battery, paperclips, a small roll of electrical tape, a length of whatever rope you prefer (550 Paracord is always a good option) and several rags. My kids keep all this in a runner's pack, though there are several other options available for them to keep their tools.

Now, no matter what you put in an EDC, it makes no difference if you don't know how to use it or what it's for. The compass, the map, and the flashlight are obvious to anyone and I think one of the first survival skills to teach your children is how to use a map and a compass. It's good in almost any emergency situation and, even without having a map available, being able to use a compass is a very good skill to have. One of the methods I used to teach my children was having a scavenger hunt around the house using only compass directions and a homemade map to each location.

If your children are a bit older (mine were 4 and 6), you can set up other challenges for them to overcome on their search. Knot tying and signaling are two I added quickly to these games, though you can add your own based on your family's needs. Remember to tailor the difficulty of the challenge to your child's abilities; you don't want them to get entirely frustrated and give up. You want them to be encouraged by early successes, as this will fuel their desire to learn more skills. Show them uses for the skills they're actively learning and they will be more eager to learn new ones. While you're teaching them about navigation, teach them how to navigate without a compass, even if it's just by using the sun to figure out direction. Making games around the skills you're teaching them has been a universally effective tool for me with young children.

Survival Items

I've covered various survival items in the preceding pages, but I know there are always some that even I forget. My wife has kindly reminded me to not forget to add these, as we've found them really helpful for us and our children. So this next section is about survival items that may not have been covered elsewhere, but which can still be very useful!

Bandanas:
These are a great multiple-use tool that I honestly believe that everyone should keep on hand.

Here are just a few things you can do with bandanas:
- They can be used as a signal by waving them.
- You can wet them in water and apply them to the back of your neck to help keep you cool.
- Wrap them over your head to prevent sunburn and heat stroke.
- Bunched up, you can use them to grab something hot (more effective if you use three or four).
- They can be used (especially with rope) as a sling. This is a David and Goliath sling, not a medical sling, though you could probably figure out a way to use them for that as well!
- You can strip them down for a short length of rope or strip them down for a longer but weaker cord.
- They can be used as a bag for gathering food or other survival objects.
- If you tie a stone in one and a rope to the other end, you can easily throw a rope where you want it.
- They easily allow you to filter particulates out of water, making it

safer to drink.

- If you tie a few stones or a large stone in one, it makes a club for self-defense.
- You can wash yourself or equipment with a clean one if you use it as a washcloth.
- They make good dust masks if worn over the face.
- They can also be cut up for their merits as fabric, clean strips of bandana are decent bandages (especially with the tampons we'll come to later for absorbency).

And that's just off the top of my head. Another good "training game" to play with your kids is to help them figure out as many uses for a bandana (or other item) as they can think of. It's a good way to get yourself into a use-everything, creative survival mindset, and you'll be surprised how ingenious some of your children's ideas are.

Balloons:

I know. They may seem odd for a child's EDC but they are another invaluable multi-use survival tool.

Balloons are watertight and remarkably elastic, you can easily carry a liter of water inside one. Though, keep in mind, when filled with a liter of water, a balloon is also very fragile, so put it inside a sock or wrap it in other fabric (one or two of the bandanas from earlier come to mind) to lessen some of the fragility aspects.

Being watertight has other uses as well. Storing things that need to stay dry is very useful, so you can carry your tinder or your matches (should you use them) in one. Also, cellphones and cameras, or anything else that you don't want to get wet.

That elasticity has other uses as well. A couple of balloons and a y-shaped branch make a decent improvised sling-shot (I recommend at least four balloons on each side though, they don't have all that much power).

Latex is flammable as well, so if you apply one of your matches to the balloon you can use it to more easily ignite your tinder.

Here's a fun fact: Did you know that you can fit your hand inside a balloon? What use does this have, you ask? Well, if you need to touch something without getting the bacteria from your most likely dirty hand on it (such as a wound, food, etc.), a balloon that hasn't been out of it's wrapper yet gives you a very crude rubber glove that is cleaner than most things you'll find. While we're on the topic of medical uses for balloons, they can make pressure bandages on the smaller parts of the body, and you can also use them to keep a wound from getting wet. (Cut on your foot? Have to walk through a dirty stream? Put the foot in a balloon.)

For slightly less practical but still useful purposes, a balloon filled with something soft (loose dirt is an option, as is native moss) makes a makeshift pillow.

Stretched over something that needs a lid, it keeps bugs, dust, and water out. See; just look at all the things you can use balloons for. And, I'm sure if you ask your children, they'll have even more ideas.

Lipstick or Crayons:
Between waterproof lipstick or crayons it's a toss-up. I like to keep one or the other on hand for marking a trail or other marking purposes, and while lipstick is easier to apply to surfaces that crayons won't mark on, the crayons are more easily flammable and I would never pass up another way to make or fuel a fire in a situation.

If you can find it (and I've had difficulty finding it and have ended up making it), dyed quality wax is a better option than crayons. However, crayons are cheaper wax which burns faster and with more smoke. Most people recommend beeswax and I am still deciding which wax I prefer though I am beginning to like soy wax for most purposes. If you do find (or make) a nice dyed wax, it has several other uses, including protecting your skin and gear from the elements (think, chapstick). Also, with bits of bandana you can make a candle from the wax and them and where a candle may not be as useful as a full-on fire, it does have its own uses (lighting my way to the bathroom if I don't want to waste my battery on a flashlight - also reading at night. (And if the size of my kids' packs allowed it, I would put a book in there too. I keep a book in my EDC but I use a bigger bag).

Paper:

Paper of some sort is useful for a lot of things, not the least of which is communication. Having the ability to leave a note for someone saying which direction you or your kids set out in when gathering food or looking for something is a useful enough thing on its own but paper also makes a better fire starter than a match, once lit. In my family we use it as gum as well - rip a piece off and chew it on the trail. Something to keep your mouth busy, stimulate saliva, and keep it from getting dry. If you're worried about an anarchic emergency situation, teach your children a simple (or not so simple) cipher to prevent your messages from being used by other eyes. I don't find it to be a useful thing to learn but my needs and emergencies are not your needs and emergencies.

Mirror:

The mirror is a dual-purpose item. First, it is an excellent long distance signaling device. Second, it can be broken for something sharp to tip an arrow or a spear. It won't do any really heavy work but something with a point you can fish or hunt with is better than nothing at all. It's no substitute for a knife but if your kids go to public school, a knife is out of the question for an EDC.

Teaching your children Morse code would be a good thing to do while you're teaching signaling. It's usable with smoke signals, tapping, or mirror flashes and is simple enough to teach to anyone. My kids learned it at the same time they were learning the Latin alphabet. We made flashcards with both of them (and a few others) on them and went through them after school.

Battery:
The 9-volt has only one real purpose (other than something heavy to tie in a bandana for rope control) and that is that when combined with the paperclip, it can produce sparks for a fire. Touch the paperclip to both of the battery's terminals (teach electricity safety here and make sure that your child's hand is insulated, even though it won't hurt them) and run it back and forth to create sparks. No substitute for matches or for my personal favorite fire starting method, a trusty butane lighter, but again, if they go to public school, your choices for what they can carry on their person at all times are hampered.

Be sure to teach fire safety before teaching them how to make fire though. A small child with reasonably easy access to fire and no restraint over when to use it is a dangerous thing. My brother got 2nd and 3rd degree burns over almost 30% of his body because he knew how to make a fire but did not know how to take care of one safely. Don't let your children make the same mistake. Start them with candles and work your way up.

Electrical Tape:

Electrical tape is a strictly personal recommendation. It is my adhesive of choice for an EDC. I prefer it to duct tape for its compression abilities, its portability, and its more precise applications. I would always keep one or the other in an EDC though. When combined with the rags, they make Band-Aids better than the ones you can find in the store.

Electrical Tape can be stretched and then it returns to its original size so it can be used to compress a wound more easily than duct tape. When thinking about urban survival, tape is invaluable and, even in wilderness survival, tape is useful. Though, unlike basically everything else in this list, it's not flammable. Though if you wrap a pan handle (or something else that gets hot that you know you'll be needing to handle) that non-flammability and insinuative quality is very useful.

Rope:

Do I even have to explain the value of rope? The reason I recommend type III paracord so highly is that it comes apart to give you eight times the length of rope you're carrying. In addition, when it's taken apart, only the nylon sheath does any real heavy lifting, so the other lines can be used as fishing lines, shoe laces, etc. It can also keep a structure together in moderate conditions.

For an everyday carry situation this is my go to rope. Though it is not ideal in all situations, it is the best overall cordage I can think of, especially Mil-spec (Though that's not to say that the cheaper commercial stuff isn't extraordinarily useful as well; in fact it's what I put in the kids' bags because it came in their favorite colors) Again, I could probably spend an entire book (maybe even two or three) on the merits of various knots, what knots to teach your kids, and how best to teach them, I'm going to avoid getting off on that tangent again. I will say: teach them a bend, a hitch, and a loop at the minimum. And, to quote something many people have said before me, "It is better to know a knot and not need it than need a knot and not know it."

Okay, so your kids have an every day carry bag but that's only one aspect of preparedness. What's next?

Your kids clearly now need to make a bug-out bag, and yes, they need to make it themselves (under your supervision of course). They will feel much more involved and take a greater interest in it if they are making it themselves.

Now, this is an area where your local school system has less to say about what they can put in this bag. Especially when working with small children (like mine were when I started this process with them), you have to take into account what they can actually carry. I could recommend a thousand products for what to carry but I don't think that's the best way to teach children how to build a BOB. They need to know what's going in it, why it's going in it, and what other uses they can have for these things. Having said that, there are seven things that every bug out bag needs, and those things are:

Hydration:
Every bag needs water and this is one of the places where a child is going to begin to have problems. Three liters of water is about seven pounds (eight, depending on what you carry it in) and where that's not much on its own, when combined with other gear (like food and a sleeping bag) and additional water for anything you have to use water to cook, it becomes a lot of weight for a little person to manage. Now, I'm not saying that you should skimp on having the little ones carry water but it is something worth taking into account.

Something my kids have taken to carrying along with water is tea bags because if we end up outside longer than our bottled water lasts, we're going to end up boiling any water we come across anyway and we may as well make tea while we're doing it.

For storing water I recommend wide-mouthed aluminum water bottles instead of plastic. Yes, they are a little heavier but much more durable and you can boil your water directly inside the bottle in a pinch. Now, I personally don't have my kids carry their own water filtration system - I'm going to make sure they stay with me and I carry one (so does the wife) but they do carry a couple of iodine tablets just in case we get separated. Not a bad idea.

Sustenance:

Food is number two on the list of things that I worried most about when thinking what to put in their bags. It had to be something light but nourishing and not need too much water to cook, otherwise it defeats the purpose. I couldn't find much of anything, other than MREs or power bars, and I didn't really want to do that, so we made hard tack. Here's how ours are made.

Step 1: Find a quality nutrition powder and a quality protein powder.
Step 2: Mix 2 parts flour to one part water with a teaspoon of salt for every cup of flour.
Step 3: Mix in protein and nutrient powders (as much as the dough will really let you incorporate) and possibly some seasonings (we like garlic powder for the savory ones and cinnamon sugar for the sweet ones).
Step 4: Bake in the oven at 375F for 45 minutes.
Step 5: Let dry in a warm dry place for at least three days; you wan the moisture gone.
Step 6: When eating, soak in liquid to soften, then consume. They're also good soaked and then pan fried, and then drink the liquid you soaked them in.

These were my first lesson with cooking with my kids, actually. Something I learned from that experience is that, especially when cooking (and I do encourage you to let your kids help you make these or just have them make them themselves by a recipe if they're a little older), is that you have to let them have room for mistakes. My six year old spilled almost five pounds of flour onto the flour while trying to get four cups into the bowl, (and I had just turned my back to check on his sister for two minutes!) and my four year old, when it came to her turn to help, set the smoke alarms off by leaving an oven mitt in the oven when we went in to check on the them cooking. Either of these incidents could have derailed the session, but I wanted to make sure my kids had a positive experience with making the tack, in case they need to do it again, by themselves someday. So accept that mistakes happen, and try to make it a fun, positive learning experience.

Clothing:
This is one of the most variable matters of a bag. Climate, taste, and season all have their factors to play in terms of what clothes you should wear but here's what we came up with for my kids.

2 pairs of shoes (the ones on their feet and the ones in the bag).
2 pairs of pants (long pants, not shorts. One of them should be reasonably warm. We lucked out and found wool pants at a thrift store).

3 shirts (2 t-shirts and a warm long sleeve shirt or sweater in the winter).

Whatever jacket is in season.

Underwear (When we first started these bags, I carried twice as much underwear and twice as many pants because my four year old was still having accidents).

A baseball cap or winter hat, depending on the season.

Three bandanas (see uses for a bandana earlier).

This is just an example. Your clothing will vary, depending on your children's ages, your location and climate, and the time of the year you are planning for.

Shelter:

This is another one where personal taste plays a big role. Some people prefer tents, others tarps, others just a waterproof bedroll. For my kids, I still keep it to a sleeping bag and a small tarp that fits inside the bag when it's rolled up. This is big enough that each can carry one and if they sleep next to each other, they're big enough to cover over them or to go underneath them. This is also dependent on climate and season though, so plan accordingly.

First Aid:

Gauze.

At least one pressure bandage.

Needle and thread (stitches could be vital. Sterilize the needle with the lighter that's going down in the fire section).

I recommend some sterile gauze and tape over prepackaged adhesive bandages for customizability of the bandage mostly. Aspirin, Acetaminophen, Ibuprofen, any daily medication, Allergy medication, Benadryl (Especially if someone has a bee allergy). Popsicle sticks for finger and toe splints.

I don't recommend a venom extractor, as from all I've been able to read they're a waste of money and space. I do however recommend a pair of high boots. Most snakebites or other creature bites happen low on the leg; a pair of high boots should prevent most, if not all, of these.

Fire:

I'm a firm believer that esoteric fire making methods (magnifying glass, battery and steel wool, soda can + chocolate bar) are all good in theory but for something as important as making a fire, and especially when surviving with kids, you want something that is going to work basically instantly every time, under any condition, and for that we turn to the humble butane lighter. Some people prefer matches but I don't like risking getting my fire making equipment wet. Everyone in my family keeps at least three lighters on them in any bug out situation. One in a pocket, one around their neck, and one in the bag.

I didn't put a pan in the kids' bags for cooking but as I mentioned before, aluminum water bottles that they can boil water in.

Light:

Flashlight, headlamp, and batteries. I personally keep a kerosene lamp but that was cut from the kids' bags for weight. Though, when they get a bit bigger they'll get one too, because it's basically a portable fire.

Weapons:

The only weapons I gave my kids were pepper spray and a safety whistle. I don't trust them with anything like a firearm at their age and they're too small for hand-to-hand combat. My wife and I considered tasers but decided against it for economy and the fact that the ones we could find ate batteries something fierce and that was extra weight for the little ones.

And finally...

They need a knife! The needs of a child for a knife are the same as an adult's. Help them pick something that will fit in their hand and realize that that measurement will change about as often as they change their shoes.

Now BOB preparation is one place where we've had a lot of luck. Our house is backed against a forest and we do three-day drills twice a year. We go out as far as the kids could walk on Friday afternoon and "get lost" and camp out of our bags for two days. Then we find our way back on Sunday night. The kids quickly learned to add a book or two to their bags (which I highly recommend for everyone but especially for children), due to the down time, but other than that, they've loved the excursions and have learned an enormous amount of skills. If you can practice in a "real-world" situation, at least by going camping, I would strongly recommend it.

So, at this point we've taught our children how to be prepared in the moment, how to run from a dangerous situation, where to meet up with us, and how to pack a bag. But in my mind, there's still one crucial aspect that's missing. That's the ability to survive for the long term in a bad situation, preferably in a central location. There are some essential skills that especially Americans have lost in the past fifty years that I feel need to make a reemergence, just in case things get bad. There are too many to go through how to teach them all to your kids here but these are some of the most needed, in my humble opinion. Feel free to disagree, change things up, or add your own that are more applicable to your family and your personal situation. Use these as a starting point for discussion with your family and go from there.

First and foremost comes the art of canning and preserving food. These are skills that have been almost entirely lost among the younger generations. Heck, even most people in my generation have no idea how to can anything (and I'm not even that old, I like to think!) And canning is not just for vegetables; you can also can meats.

Now I'm not saying you should entirely neglect purchasing cans of goods, as they are cheaper, more durable, and more readily available but in even a couple of weeks in a regional survival situation, the cans are eventually going to run out and being able to make your own would be a great boon if you wanted to go "off the grid". They would be invaluable come winter when your crops are no longer producing, and they are a great skill to teach your children.

Now, why do I place canning above gardening or hunting? You can find abundant food in the outside world in the spring, summer, and autumn. You can trade for it and you can (if needed) steal it but in the winter there is never enough natural food to go around and having a supply of your own that is safe through the winter is an invaluable resource. And, if you're particularly good at this skill, you can trade your canning skill into something else valuable by offering to can food that people bring you for some other service.

The value of storable food is something we often underrate in our modern mega-mart society but I have lived in the Northwest long enough and have been rained or snowed in often enough to realize that there's not always easy access to food, even without a disaster of some sort to complicate matters further.

This is one of the rare times in one of my books where I will make a product recommendation and say that everyone seriously interested in the subject should pick up a copy of the Ball Blue Book of Preserving and practice working from it. You can find a lot of this information online as well but the book would be an incredibly invaluable commodity should we have a societal collapse (I also just like having physical media on hand, especially in the kitchen). There are several other good books to have on hand but you can get this one for less than ten dollars and it is well worth it.

I'm a very big believer in getting kids into the kitchen, so help walk them through the recipes and techniques and then have them make them themselves. The skills you can learn from canning (knifework, cook times, and sanitation among others) are useful in all aspects of cooking and being able to cook is a valuable skill in any situation, emergency or not.

Other emergency cooking skills worth learning and teaching include smoking and curing meat. Curing meat is easy, though you need either curing salt (pink salt - you can find it online or in specialty stores) or celery/spinach juice (some other leafy green vegetable juice will also do the job here).

There are countless recipes online for smoking and curing your own meat. I prefer brining (that is wet curing) to dry curing. I find the seasonings penetrate the meat better. However, dry curing is often easier. Remember that you're going to want to add more than just salt to your curing or your meat will just taste like salt. Something sweet will help cut that saltiness a lot (honey and brown sugar are traditional). One of my favorite chefs brines his turkeys before roasting them for Thanksgiving dinner. Here's an example.

His recipe for a 14lb turkey is:
1 cup kosher salt
1/2 cup light brown sugar
1 gallon vegetable stock
1 tablespoon black peppercorns
1 1/2 teaspoons allspice berries
1 1/2 teaspoons chopped candied ginger
1 gallon heavily iced water

Now I recommend that you make sure your meat is in smaller, more manageable and storable portions, but you can brine an entire turkey whole - it will take longer to cure than smaller pieces though.

Brining is an easy one to practice with your kids. I use a scaled down version of that recipe for roasting chickens and we do that about once every two weeks. We set it in the brine in the morning and put it in the oven at 4:30PM (I like to roast my birds at high heat ,so we put them on at 500-600F degrees, depending on what sort of oven you have. My minimum roasting temp is 450F; it gives you a much juicier bird than the traditional 350.) Now, a one-day brine is not long enough to properly cure meat but it teaches your children the method, which is the important thing. We've eaten cured pork two years after preserving with no ill effects but always make sure that you cure safely, with proper sanitation and be sure to get your sodium nitrite in there. Botulism is a very, very ugly thing.

Something that I have never seen happen, but I have had other people who have cured meats and all of my old curing books tell me about, is that a small amount of white mold may grow on your preserved meat after some time. This is harmless and prevents more dangerous molds from taking root. If it were to occur on my meat, I would probably cut the outer layer off (just because I'm very squeamish about bacteria) and serve the rest. If anything green grows on your meat, get rid of it; there is no saving it.

Now, for a bit of black magic. No, not really. Did you know the Egyptians had functional refrigeration thousands of years before electricity? (History lesson with your kids here). Now, think about that for a moment. How they did it was reasonably simple and is an excellent opportunity to teach your children science they wouldn't otherwise learn until college. It's also a good family weekend project to make a few of these and let the kids experiment with them. (I put one each in the kids' bedrooms to keep the water they like to keep by their bed cold)

Here's what you'll need.
- 2 clay pots (UNGLAZED) - the smaller one needs to fit inside the larger one, with some room around it. Be sure to plug any holes that are in the bottom of the pots (as you're most likely to find unglazed clay pots as flower pots and they have holes in their bottoms) - clay, epoxy, cork, large rocks, or my personal preferred, electrical tape will plug these holes quite effectively.
- Sand (reasonably coarse sand works better here but anything will do.)
- Water

You take the large pot and fill it with enough sand so that the top of the smaller pot will sit at the same height with the top of the larger one. Then you place the smaller one inside and fill the gap between the two pots with sand, leaving a small portion unfilled (about a finger's width from the top). Take water and wet the sand between the two and cover the top of the inner pot with a wet cloth until it gets cold. Then, just keep the pots in a warm, dry place and evaporation will do the chilling for you. You'll have to make sure the sand stays wet (this requires adding water about twice a day)

The children loved making these and believed they were magic until I explained the science of thermal exchange to them. Not a long-term preservation solution but I love having mine to keep things cool without the need for electricity. They are rather water intensive though so only use them in an area where water is plentiful. I've kept uncured meat in one of these things for over a week (ten days, I think) and they keep water icy cold for drinking.

One point on which I will probably be in the minority with almost every other guide you will read is on the point of hunting and self-defense. I don't believe that guns are your best choice here, necessarily. They are loud, cumbersome, and their ammunition cannot be easily home-made or found (because in an emergency situation, the gun store is going to get raided extremely quickly).

On the other hand, I am a very firm believer in learning how to make bows, crossbows, and slings, and becoming proficient in their use. Crossbows are good if you're used to guns, though a bow is often the better choice for children who don't have that built in muscle memory that many of the adults who will be teaching them will have in terms of shooting. Now, this is a point where I am definitely saying MAKE YOUR OWN and teach your children to make their own: Arrows. Knowing how to make and use arrows will give you a nearly limitless source of ammunition long after the last bullet has been fired.

Guns do have their uses and if you have the money to purchase a few shotguns and their ammunition, that is not a bad option, but for most emergency purposes, a bow will do you as well, if not better, than a handgun or small caliber rifle.

You can make a bow in the following way: Take about a four-foot piece of a hardwood (oak is a decent starter - a 48inch by 1/2inch piece of trim from your local hardware store works wonderfully) and a two-foot piece of soft wood (poplar is a good one), wood glue and rope. You will also need a planer or a knife.

Glue the softwood to the hardwood with your wood glue, place the softwood in the center of your hardwood beam (remember that it should be twice as long) and tie or clamp it in place.

Once the glue has set (at least overnight), plane the bow down. You want it to taper from thin to thick with another thin point in the middle (the handle), almost like two opposing teardrops. It's very important that you make sure that both sides of the bow are even.

Then, cut notches out for the string. They should be a few inches from the top and bottom of your bow

Once the bow is strung, check the draw strength. If it's too hard to draw back to full extension, you'll need to plane more to thin the bow and weaken the draw strength. There's no real way to increase the draw strength of a bow that I know of, so it's better to reduce it progressively than to go too far the other way.

There are several good resources on how to tiller a bow. That is to make sure it draws well and evenly without having to go back and replane it two dozen times. It is the subject of it's own treatise and not something that can (or should) be covered in this book. Though I said to use a 48-inch piece earlier, don't forget to adjust the size to the size of your child. You never want to fire a bow taller than you are.

Be sure to keep a longbow unstrung when not in use; you don't want them to take a permanent curve or they lose power, though if you make a compound bow (and that is a very technically demanding piece of craft), you don't have that worry.

Don't neglect armed melee combat in terms of self-defense. So many people I know seem content with learning a martial art and ignore the fact that many of their attackers will be better armed. I have been teaching my kids from ancient fighting manuals (mostly maces and axes) that are available online. We all practice against each other with properly weighted weapons coated in thick foam.

It's great fun and it has allowed us to work against moving and resisting targets without risk of hurting each other too terribly.

The reason I recommend axe and mace combat above using a sword or a machete is long-term access to them. Most of my family's prepping is for natural disasters and societal collapse and in a societal collapse situation you need to be able to make your own tools and it's very technically demanding to make a functional sword. An axe, spear, or mace is far simpler to produce and easier to learn to use. Anyone can use a mace with a reasonable level of proficiency; it's no different than swinging a bat around. Knife combat is something that could be worth teaching as well but I've always preferred to have a reach advantage against an enemy.

There are many, many other skills worth learning, and maybe I'll have to write a couple more books on them all! Among them are brewing (beer is a valuable commodity and it is a safe liquid to drink, the brewing process kills bacteria), basic construction, especially if you use the ancient Japanese techniques of constructing without nails or stone construction (very useful, just in case nails become a scarce resource).

Something else that is often overlooked is learning to tell stories and play an instrument. It's something to keep the mind busy in any situation. Learn to amuse yourself without the need for electronics or even without outside tools at all. It's often made the difference in our own lives between a hopeless and boring trip back home and a lively happy one. It is also a tool you can always barter with.

The value of a basic scientific education is often underrated as well - biology, chemistry, and physics (especially the physics related to the laws of motion and how energy is transferred) is very useful in a survival situation. Of course, learning what food is edible and what isn't should be on the list, though remember that if you're in an area where you are unfamiliar with the local plants, you're going to need to do research on what is safe and what isn't. It is always better to do this in a time when you don't need it than in a time when you do.

Something else to mention is to get involved with other preppers in your area. Especially ones with kids - it gives you a social connection, gives your kids someone to play with, and you can all teach them and each other different skills that others may not have. We learned to make bows from a family that I met on a prepper website that happened to live in my local area. Moderately sized groups will be able to get more done than several smaller ones as well and if you can band together with others in your area you will be better off than just your family alone. Just make sure that they are people you can rely on and not ones that will leech off you if things get bad.

Also, it's worth thinking about children when stockpiling goods. If you have children, or even if you don't, it may be worth getting baby supplies to trade or use for yourself. Children aren't going to stop existing in an emergency, and if you have diapers when all those around you have run out you, are going to be a hero and highly in demand. Same with baby formula or jars of baby food.

Some of the other things my children have taught me to stock up on are books and cards. The kids were talking to some ex-military people who told them that a deck of cards or a good book was one of the best things you could get in a care package. It got us to thinking about that sort of thing in an emergency - even if it's just a citywide power outage, having card and board games could be a wonderful trading commodity and source of entertainment. Most of the stockpiling my family does is for trade though; we trust ourselves to be mostly self-sufficient in terms of food and other things like that.

The final note I will leave you with is how to best teach all this, and more, to children.

Step 1: Allow them to make mistakes. Mistakes are the price we pay for growth. You cannot expect children to understand something the first time and get it right away. Some will understand some things immediately but there will be other things that they will struggle with. Learn the skills yourself and learn them several different ways so that if a child isn't grasping it one way, they can try another. (This last point is true of all education and it is worth remembering that there almost always multiple ways to accomplish something; let them find their own way to do it)

Step 2: Explain not just the *how* but the *why*. This was something my wife and I learned with food preparation. Our children knew that they needed to keep a sanitary workstation when canning but they didn't know *why* and so they often forgot and contaminated what they were working with. Now there are two ways to handle this: you can either punish them until they just stop forgetting or you can explain to them why it's important and once they truly understand, they will often be more aware of the need to do it. It has worked with my children for everything from school work to sanitation and I swear by teaching my children why we do things instead of just how we do things and if I cannot adequately explain why something is done the way it's done, I clearly don't know enough about it to be teaching it!

Step 3: Make it fun. This is something I learned when writing children's' educational books and applied to my own children. They're much more likely to grasp something and remember it, if it's enjoyable. I found when I was teaching music that the kids who enjoyed their instruments made more progress than the ones who did not, and part of that is that they practiced more. If you can slip preparation training into a game, you've won.

It really is that simple to teach children almost anything. Let them learn these things in a non-emergency situation so that they have them in case of an emergency.

Hopefully this book has provided some food for thought on a skill or two that maybe you had overlooked. I hope you find prepping with your children to be a rewarding and educational experience. Hopefully the day never comes that your children will need the lifesaving skills that you have taught them, but you should sleep better at night knowing that your children are capable of taking care of themselves and helping those around them.

Sign up for Robert's Mailing List to be notified of **New Releases** and **Special Sales**: http://eepurl.com/zvm11

No Spam – he promises!

If you've enjoyed this book, please **leave a review** and let us know your thoughts!

Other Books by Robert Paine:

The Survivalist Cookbook - Recipes for Preppers
Prepping for Survival: 65 Supplies You Need to Live Through Anything
Survival Kit Essentials: 10 Things to Keep You Alive
The Dead Road: The Complete Collection